The Author

Dr. William Kent Larkin is a researcher specializing in applied neuroscience with the integration of positive psychology and quantum physics. Dr. Larkin works in helping individuals and organizations create an UpSpiral, find their strengths and to build a central vision or aim based upon them. His specialty is creating and maintaining what he calls an "UpSpiral" of positivity which enriches individual lives and promotes and increases organizational productivity. His research indicates that when people live in an UpSpiral, the process of personal discovery he outlines here unfolds, creates clarity of aim and self-definition. Within this process, he has invented what he has trademarked, "The Emotional Gym".

"We are a culture driven by trying to change our weaknesses, when actually our weaknesses change very little over a lifetime. That window of change is only 3%, at the most 7%. In contrast, our ability to sustain an UpSpiral of positivity has a natural tendency to engage unique personal strengths which have infinite malleability. Personal strengths can grow enormously, and when they do, they undo weaknesses, they heal weaknesses, and they manage weaknesses by creating new goals, personal clarity, direction, vision and even revelation," contends Dr. Larkin. He believes that we would develop many more prodigies and geniuses if we focused on creating an UpSpiral of positive emotion and mood, rather than on "balance", "wholeness" and fixing weaknesses.

With a degree from Yale University, and a doctorate in psychology and religion from Harvard University, he has also done post-doctoral work in neuroscience and holds a Certificate in neuropsychology. Dr. Larkin was, for 10 years, the voice of psychology for the Armed Forces Network which broadcast to 72 countries of the world. **Breakthrough with Dr. Larkin,** both radio and television, won 62 national and international awards including the New York City International Festival of Radio Gold Medal and 2 Gabriel Awards from the United States Catholic Communicators Association.

The PM Factor Test

A Test of the Positive Mind

The PM Factor Test has emerged from my work with my clients and seminars. It is a subjective measure which gives an important indication of where you see yourself on these dimensions of the test. It is used to chart movement and growth over time.

Take the test before you read the book, then take the test again, after you have read the book and done the exercises. If you want, you can take it somewhere in the middle. When you have finished the book and the exercises, send your scores to us and we will tell you what they tell us.

Your subjective sense of where you are on this measure is fundamentally important, because what you believe to be true about your own positive mind is strikingly accurate. What we believe about ourselves, particularly in terms of our positive mind, conditions our perceptions and those perceptions affect how we feel and behave. When beliefs and thoughts change, behavior changes, as it relates to the positive mind.

The real power of the process I introduce here is not in huge leaps of growth and in big doses of joy or happiness; it is rather in a slowly, daily, "lean" in the direction of becoming more and more positive, of growing in the UpSpiral, which you will come to understand.

If you went to a gym to get physically in shape, the trainer would not give the heaviest weights to lift first; you would start with the smaller ones and build your strength. It is the same with positive "emotional muscle". Start with the small shifts of consciousness that will come to mean everything. Grow a little at a time and appreciate the value of small incremental changes of positive feelings, over a period of time.

Learning to "savor" is more important in the long run, than learning to "jump for joy". I promise you, if you get good at savoring your life, over time, you will "jump for joy" much more often.

So be kind to yourself, be gentle, love the emerging positive self that you really, essentially are; a wonderful package of significant and unique strengths that you will discover, as you proceed here. This is meant to be enjoyable. If it gets to be burdensome, drop back a little, to where it is easy and don't worry about time or progress. Just work at it at your own speed, with a little consistent determination. As you learn to "feel good", that "feeling good" will motivate you to feel even better.

I have great confidence in you.

ANI

The Applied Neuroscience Institute

www.gotoani.com

In addition to this book ANI Offers

Seminars

Workshops

Individual Consulting

Organizational Consulting

Certification Training

The Positive Mind Test

12 Step UpSpiraLife Groups

The UpSpiraLife Foundation

The NeuroPositive™ Life Coach Certificate

The NeuroPositive™ Life Coach License

The NeuroPositive™ Recovery Coach

The NeuroPositive™ CareTaker Coach

The Satsang NeuroPositive™ Coach

The NeuroPositive™ 12 Step Group Coach

The NeuroPositive™ Zipline (Continuing Education)

GROWING THE POSITIVE MIND: The Emotional Gym

PRINTED IN THE UNITED STATES OF AMERICA

ISBN 978-1-60585-017-7

First Printing 2008
Second Printing 2009
Third Printing 2010
Fourth Printing 2011
Fifth Printing 2012
Sixth Printing 2013
Seventh Printing 2014

Neuroscience Press
PRINTED IN THE UNITED STATES OF AMERICA

www.appliedneuroscienceinstitute.com
www.gotoani.com

To Dr. Elkhonon Goldberg

Inspired teacher
Ingenious researcher
Mentor of mentors

Nick Goldberg was a student of Alexandr Luria, the father of neuropsychology, in Russia. He brought much of neuropsychology to this country. He is a Clinical Professor of Neurology at the New York University School of Medicine and a Diplomate of the American Board of Professional Psychology. He was my teacher, supervisor, and mentor.

He is one of the foremost authorities on the frontal lobes in the world today.

Contents

Introduction To Growing The Positive Mind And The NeuroPositive Method™

This book is for normal, everyday people with the everyday issues of life. It is written for anyone to understand, whether or not you have a background in neuroscience or psychology. It is not written, nor is it a prescription for people with mental health problems, though it may be helpful to them. This is a book for normal people, with normal everyday problems who want to feel better, be happier, and feel like they fit more into their own skin. It is for people who want to grow in their lives without feeling like they have to be analyzed, "psychologized," labeled, healed or diagnosed in order to feel better. It for people who want to feel good without having to work through all their past issues or their problems, and who do not want to spend endless time (and money) talking about or focusing on their weaknesses and what needs fixing or healing.

This is a book about growing from normal to better and best in a way that is simple, healthy and that works. It is not written to discourage those who need mental health services, counseling, therapy, or medication for mental illness. There is surely that need— even a crisis for those who are most in need of those services and cannot secure them. It is not the intention to discourage those who give or need services for mental illness issues. There are good doctors and therapists who will be sure that you grow beyond your problems, and there are bad ones that will keep you too focused for too long on what is wrong with you and what needs to be healed, with no real solutions.

Negativity can be an addiction as surely as people can be addicted to almost anything or anyone. Those with addiction issues may find the material here to be helpful after they have grown past their dependency upon substances, sex, gambling, relationships, or whatever, but not as a substitute for that very necessary process of recovery from addiction when it is needed.

The NeuroPositive Method, which is explained here, is for positive growth. It is positive growth that is at the heart of who we are, and it is a much more rapid way of growth than focusing on weaknesses, issues or problems. We live in a culture that is massively influenced by what is wrong and what is negative. We have billion dollar industries with an enormous focus on "fixing," finding solutions, healing and solving problems. There is so much focus on what is negative that we have become too influenced by focusing on the negative and what is wrong. That focus creates a particular kind of growth in the brain that is negative, pessimistic, and creates many of the mental illness issues that are prevalent today. This degree of negativity creates the wrong focus and asks the wrong questions. Rather than ask, "what creates illness?" the question here is "what creates health?"

We are too full of angst and dread and a growing epidemic of depression. We are too influenced by diagnostic labels, drugs with too many side-effects that don't do what they promise, and that have been inadequately or dishonestly researched. We have made too many normal things in life psychological issues that do not need a therapist or counselor, that do not need medication. We respond best to the normal on-going process of life as the primary source of healing. There is too much over-diagnosis and too many pills with questionable research to justify their use for too many people who don't really need them, get no exercise, and eat too much of the wrong foods.

Can you imagine a time when a psychiatrist would tell a mild to moderately depressed client that they would not get an anti-depressant until they had sufficient physical exercise and a very healthy diet? Or even ask questions about proper diet and exercise? How many people, obese from a cocktail of ineffective medications, would have profited from a discipline of yoga everyday?

Treatment in the mental illness business begins with a diagnosis and the assignment of a label that is an indicator of what is considered abnormal, in need of repair and healing. It is given a number and a name based upon the DSM V. The process that follows is therapy. On every level, this constitutes the admission that something is wrong and needs to be fixed. This has developed a decided lean in creating a nation of victims— people who believe that something causes what they do and makes them less responsible. Whatever this is, there is the belief that some process or medication or both will relieve the core problem or problems. In some cases, where there is genuine illness, this can be helpful and provide proven results. In many other cases, it has failed to create short or long-term change. Is there any challenge in life that will not someday be included in the DSM? This is the diagnostic manual of the American Psychiatric Association, used by those who diagnose and treat mental illness.

What has occurred is that working through normal problems

and issues of life has come to be considered a part of the business of treating mental illness, and that is just not accurate. More and more problems and issues in normal and everyday life have been cast within the realm of diagnosis and treatment. The more this realm is increased, the more everyday issues become issues cast into a medical model. This book is about a process that recasts much of this medicalization of problems into the realm of education and training.

We have been too conditioned to believe that the past must be repaired in every case and instance for life to move on. Those who choose this particular journey are convinced that everyone must travel as they have. Just as sure are those who make an income from "healing" and those who hold power by sustaining the myth of necessary and required suffering, whether they are mental illness professionals or ministers. We are much more likely to repair the parts of the past that really need it when we have grown in the strengths and the ways that truly enable us to look back and know what needs attention, and what can best be left behind and better left alone. Even in the various 12 step movements, three steps of growth are necessary before "character weaknesses" begin to be addressed.

We have believed too much in suffering as a necessary part of growth, and that growth and health depend upon a sufficient diet of negative experience from which strength emerges by navigating problems. Strengths already exist within us before life's problems and suffering have ever been navigated. Sin is not nearly so "original" or inherent as some proclaim it to be, in order to sustain their crumbling meaning making scheme. The school of "hard knocks" is only one way and not "the" way.

We have been led to believe that opposites are necessary to

deepen experience. Joy is joy and misery is not a requirement to know joy. Love is love and we do not have to experience the depth of loss to know love. We have been led to believe that suffering is so necessary that we feel guilt when accomplishment comes easily and in the "flow" of following our passion. We have plumbed the depths of these beliefs about suffering and the importance of great trials of life; we have not paid nearly enough attention to lives that have done well without a great deal of suffering and to those who have been successful without a life filled with misery. It is not necessary to have a life crippled with loss and loneliness to write a great love story or to live a life filled with love. We have just paid too much attention, too long, to the myths of the masculine journey that no longer serve our evolution, as we get better at looking at successful businesses, marriages and individual lives that have thrived. We are beginning to allow the feminine, women, and the right hemisphere of the brain to teach us more and more, and to begin forming a new mythology not nearly so filled with the journey of the "hero" and "his" mountains that must be conquered.

We are pretty good at fixing some things that don't work; we are not nearly so good at paying closer attention to what works well and building upon it. While we learn from our mistakes, we learn much more from what makes us achieve and be successful. We can be much better at insuring the probability of succeeding in grade school in a way that creates real self-esteem from having done esteeming things. Too much time has been spent rationalizing the good that comes from suffering as a necessity for growth, rather than discovering and sustaining the strengths of the person that more likely insure success. Very, very early we have taught children what is wrong with them that must be corrected rather than how these small children's emerging strengths can be nurtured into genius. We have medicated children and teenagers with Ritalin and

bi-polar treatments that have addicted them to medications as surely as illegal street drugs. Could it be that the war on drugs should
be directed more at pharmaceutical companies in this country than
drug lords in South America? We grow genius by recognizing and
growing what is good, not from correcting what is wrong before we
can get started with what is good. A child prodigy emerges from a
child's strengths recognized and nurtured.

The NeuroPositive Method is not about diagnosis, which con-
notes illness, and it is not about treatment of an illness or something
that is wrong. The process here is education, not therapy. This
begins with the assumption that we start with what is good and what
works, build upon that, and go from there. We do not start with the
assumption that something is wrong, but we also we do not assume
that people know what they want. We do assume that people may
think that they know what they want, but that oftentimes what people might think are their goals, vaguely or fairly clearly, will not
give them what they expect that the fulfillment of these goals will
deliver. The emerging life coaching industry is misguided in
encouraging goal-setting without the significant education that
needs to occur before goals are formed and pursued that will not
bring fulfillment or satisfaction.

The NeuroPositive process begins with building an UpSpiral,
finding and increasing information about personal strengths, and
some considerable time spent in the state of "flow" as an expression
one's personal vibration –in that order. Then goals may be clarified and formed, later refined into a vision for living that provides
a sense of personal significance and personal meaning making.
Clear and focused but malleable goals along with a personal sense
of significance and authentic meaning making increase resilience
and thriving in life. The absence of these essential building blocks

has caused what seems to be illness in many people. There are stages and transitions in life that are a part of the natural developmental process. If growth through these stages is not made, what looks like illness occurs. The refusal to face these transitions between these stages is a major cause of the problems and issues of normal development that come to be labeled as illness. When we educate people to know what these normal stages of life and the transitions between them look like, we chart a course of growth, while very idiosyncratic and individual, which has common themes of a life-long developmental cycle. The stages of life after 40 are as significant developmentally as those that have come before 20. We are not as fixed by the past as we have come to believe. We are more formed by the present and the sense of personal significance we create in it that navigates future ways of making meaning. This future is far more compelling and powerful than trudging through the past before enough strength has been developed to make sense or meaning of it. Those who live the longest are those involved in meaning making and long-term expansive perspectives in life that provide a sense of personal significance.

The NeuroPositive Method works on the basis of the reality of an unfolding and potentially always evolving brain and mind. Neuroplasticity is never still, neither when we are awake nor when we sleep. Every thought we think and every feeling we feel is adding to these developing neuropathways. We are beginning to be aware that we can be much more mindful of our thoughts and feelings, and this increasing mindfulness can recapture our sense of mastery and quiet, an easy inner power that is the opposite of being a victim of one's issues or problems.

There are those who journey through these life-long developmental stages more easily and successfully than others. We have just not paid much attention to them. The framework provided here is designed to provide education that sustains this movement through stages and transitions. When this evolution is blocked by a fixed determination to remain too long in one stage of life, and there is a push against transition to the next, then confusion and a lost sense of personal significance creates the illnesses that are signs of this resistance. Major transitions in life create an increased sense of a loss of personal significance and threaten the already existing meaning making system of the person. Movement through a transition is often personally difficult to sustain without the support that comes from education and compassionate personal understanding, often sustained in the strength of one's community. My book which follows this one, **12 New Steps of a New Millennium: The UpSpiraLife Group,** outlines a group process that provides this kind of support in a group or community. This book describes the more general approach I have come to call NeuroPositive.™

The NeuroPositive Method builds upon the innate capacity of the individual to create and sustain an UpSpiral that sustains future growth. Learn to sustain this UpSpiral and personal significance and meaning making will follow. The first step is creating awareness and understanding of how to sustain this positive growth that creates this UpSpiral, while the remainder of the steps uphold and sustain what Dr. Barbara Fredrickson has discovered and named the "Broaden and Build Theory." The wide array of "Broaden and Build" research in the medical field, psychology and neuroscience is the basis of what has hopefully been expressed here as an easily understood and workable method I have called NeuroPositive.

Focus on the negative and your brain will grow the negative. Focus on what is good and the nature of your brain is most effectively utilized at what is at the heart of the NeuroPositive Method:

the brain is designed to grow best in a positive way. **Growing the Positive Mind** is about neuroplasticity. We know now that the brain is a not a fixed organ, that it is continually evolving, and that the neuropathways in the brain are formed by what we think about, what we feel, and then how what we give our attention to is perceived by the brain we have been busy creating.

So let's be busy creating a positive brain, which is what the brain is most like in its basic nature. Let's grow neuropathways in the brain, called neuroplasticity, that can create a more positive, more fit, more resilient brain. That is what we call NeuroPositive. That is the process you will learn about here. I call them promises because they work, if you do them.

We begin here with an UpSpiral.™ Everything in the NeuroPositive Method™ unfolds from the establishment of this UpSpiral. You will learn in my Emotional Gym™ that it is ok to feel positive emotions for no reason at all, and you will learn how to grow them in three essential dimensions. The emotions from this gym will feel better than big pecs or breast implants.

Then you will learn through scientific testing that you have strengths that will keep you in an UpSpiral if you validate them, use them, and grow them in new ways. Many of these strengths are those you take for granted or that you may not have recognized at all. Using these strengths appropriately and with savvy makes you happier.

This will put you into a place where you are ready to experience "flow" in your life. The concept of flow is actually a vibration that can change your approach to life and make you more successful at feeling good most of the time, and help you feel better when things seem to go wrong in life. It is meditation and mindfulness "on the move." From there, I take you into the process of setting some long-term but very malleable five-year goals. The brain works best from specificity; it grows from "getting it together" then letting go and unfolding, moving into higher structures of "getting it together" again and again. Your brain is made for transitions in life; your brain is never a stagnant organ.

We will move then to creating a sense of personal significance, a core issue in mental vitality and resilience. This is about vision in life. I am not a great proponent of the purpose-driven life, because I believe that life should be inspired rather than driven. We are already too driven. Get a vision that gives you a sense of personal significance and you will attract the people that will help you move your vision along and increase and enrich your sense of being a part of something significant.

The NeuroPositive Method has two primary goals at its core:
1. to feel good most of the time
2. to feel a sense of significance in the gift of life that you create

Before you begin reading more here about the NeuroPositive method and its exercises, take the "Positive Mind Test" on the back cover, and then again in a few months after you have completed all of the exercises. See how you score then and how your life has changed in a more satisfying and vital way.

Growing a positive mind is the lubricant of the neuroplasticity that will change both your mind and your brain. In doing so, you will raise your happiness set-point, your emotional set-point, your sense of personal significance, and your authentic meaning making. You will create more of what you really want in a process that is the normal experience of a resilient and thriving life.

Growing
The Positive
Mind

with the   Emotional Gym

and the   Positive Mind Test

by Dr. William K. Larkin

Neuroscience
Press

The PM Factor

A Test of the Positive Mind
Circle one: 1 = none or little true, 10 = very true

1. I experience a positive energy that
   others notice and that is infectious.   1-2-3-4-5-6-7-8-9-10

2. I can help others see the positive in
   negative situations and often do so.   1-2-3-4-5-6-7-8-9-10

3. It doesn't take me long in the face of
   a situation that seems negative,
   to find something good.   1-2-3-4-5-6-7-8-9-10

4. I can stay positive for a long time
   before a difficult situation works out.   1-2-3-4-5-6-7-8-9-10

5. I have developed definite strategies and
   tools to maintain a positive attitude.   1-2-3-4-5-6-7-8-9-10

6. I don't let much get me down.   1-2-3-4-5-6-7-8-9-10

7. In a group of people, I tend to be the
   most positive in the bunch.   1-2-3-4-5-6-7-8-9-10

8. I am able to soothe myself and be
   good to me.   1-2-3-4-5-6-7-8-9-10

9. I practice random acts of kindness
to myself. 1-2-3-4-5-6-7-8-9-10

10. I have a sense of direction and purpose. 1-2-3-4-5-6-7-8-9-10

11. I feel like life has a significance and
meaning, that it is forward-moving in
a positive way. 1-2-3-4-5-6-7-8-9-10

12. Joy is an easy feeling for me to have. 1-2-3-4-5-6-7-8-9-10

13. Confidence is an easy feeling for me
to have. 1-2-3-4-5-6-7-8-9-10

14. Love is an easy feeling for me to have. 1-2-3-4-5-6-7-8-9-10

15. I have at least 3 different networks of
friends and acquaintances. 1-2-3-4-5-6-7-8-9-10

16. I notice good things in other people
before I notice the negative. 1-2-3-4-5-6-7-8-9-10

17. When I make a mistake, I look at the
situation until I learn whatever lesson
it has to teach me, then I let go of it. 1-2-3-4-5-6-7-8-9-10

18. I have some pretty specific
long-term goals. 1-2-3-4-5-6-7-8-9-10

19. I have projects in my life that absorb
my attention and I love doing them. 1-2-3-4-5-6-7-8-9-10

20. I have a personal guru, a guide, or a
    coach who helps point me in the right
    direction and helps me hold myself
    accountable.   1-2-3-4-5-6-7-8-9-10

Add the total number of your individual scores.   _____

Go to **www.positivemindtest.com**, take the PM Factor test there, and receive a free analysis of your score.

Dr. William K. Larkin
Copyright 2008

www.AppliedNeuroscienceInstitute.com

The Emotional Gym

**You can feel the positive emotions
that you choose to feel
if you lean your consciousness
consistently and gently over time
in that positive direction.**

You exercise your body, you exercise your brain, you do spiritual exercises and you seek to control what you can control in order to feel good and make things work. Why do you never think of exercising your emotions? Particularly the good ones –practice them so that while you are feeling them, they grow stronger, and last longer and are easier to get to.

Because we tend to think that emotions just happen to us, it is not always apparent to us that we create our emotions, and that we can utilize, direct, and control our emotional states and moods.

Your brain likes to be happy. It really does want to feel good; it evolves better. In fact, your brain does its best work when you are in a positive state. It craves the synchronicity and rhythm that feeling good provokes by decreasing the unnecessary use of psychic energy away from conflict. Instead, it channels it to more broad-based creativity and more efficient and effective problem solving. Your brain seems to follow a kind of law of attraction; the more it feels good, the more good feeling it will build and attract, basically for evolutionary purposes. The potential for the brain to grow is best when you are in a positive state of mind. It "hums" better, it's more creative.

Because we tend to think that emotions just happen to us, it is not always apparent to us that we create our emotions, and that we can utilize, direct, and control our emotional states and moods.

This is about growing emotional muscle. That's what the *Emotional Gym* is about; building strong, reflexive, emotional muscles that give you greater control over your emotions, your emotional states and your emotional moods - particularly the good ones. That emotional muscle will help you grow a strong positive mind. It sounds like something your mother used to tell you, doesn't it? Strong muscles build a strong body. Here it is again, in a little different form; emotional muscle builds a strong positive mind and consequently, better health.

It is this emotional muscle that will keep you in the *UpSpiral*. Isn't that what you want the most: to "feel good"? That is exactly what happens in the *UpSpiral*. Here's the formula. Develop emotional muscle, stay in the *UpSpiral*, grow a positive mind and "feel good". If feeling good is what you want (and don't kid yourself that it isn't), then here is how to do it.

Developing physical muscle at a gym involves gaining a greater degree of conscious control over the physical body. The *Emotional Gym* gives a greater degree of conscious control over your emotions, your emotional state, your moods, and your state of mind. State of Mind Management (SOMM) is what the *Emotional Gym* is really all about. Remember: you have the power to exert conscious control over your emotions and how you can gain that control.

A large part of this control is in growing positive emotion. It is well within your ability to master three essential aspects of positive emotion that will be covered in detail throughout this book:
1. Immediacy –getting to the emotion instantly
2. Duration –being able to make an emotion last over time
3. Intensity –being able to increase the amplitude of an emotion.

An increased bank account or reserve (a buffer) of positive emotions will make you more resistant to negative emotions. This reservoir of practiced emotion will reduce the "staying power" of negative emotions. Build your reservoir and you will get rid of negative emotions more quickly.

The *Emotional Gym* will give you more conscious control over emotions, especially positive ones. Grow these positive emotions and they will hold your negative ones in check in turn. These positive emotions are the major part of what will give you conscious control of your emotional states. It's really pretty simple. Increase your access to positive emotions, develop this ability through practice, and the result will be fewer negative emotions. An increased bank account or reserve (a buffer) of positive emotions will make you more resistant to negative emotions. This reservoir of practiced emotion will reduce the "staying power" of negative emotions. Build your reservoir and you will get rid of negative emotions more quickly. When you have a strong, toned, muscular body, you reap the benefits by feeling better; in turn, you probably eat far less junk food. When you have strong positive emotions that you can readily draw upon because you have learned to access them, you are less willing to engage or tolerate negative emotional states. You'll feel better and make better choices.

A great deal of attention has been given to "thinking" correctly with the idea that thoughts control feelings. That is only partially true. Feelings also create thinking and thought patterns, especially negative ones. Some feelings are the result of thinking; many others are the result of the fact that we have a sensory system that was in place, both in terms of evolution and in terms of the self, before thinking became more predominant.

Millions of years before we were thinking organisms, we were in our evolution collectively and individually sensing, feeling, and intuiting organisms. The brain's frontal lobes and their executive functions emerged only much later. In other words, we had a thalamic feeling/sensing/intuitive brain for millions of years before the thinking functions of the frontal lobes and their executive functions evolved. We have not, however, evolved nearly so far as some science would lead us to believe. Our frontal lobes have not replaced, by any means, the feeling, sensing and intuiting functions of the thalamic brain. The nature of the thalamus and its complex role in both processing and integrating sensory input and its connection to the frontal lobes is discussed by Goldberg in **The Executive Brain** (page 30) in much greater detail.

However, the evolutionary task today, in which we are all engaged, involves a balance or 'coming into alignment' of the proficiency of the frontal lobes with the "earthy" power of the thalamic brain. In our tendency to "over think," the thalamic brain reasserts its claims to deeper and different functions of the integration and action process. It is important to understand the need to quiet the frontal lobes and to listen more deeply and differently to the messages of the rest of the brain, as in meditation. Even our science has not caught up with this balancing, evolving brain.

Thinking, as we define it narrowly today, certainly has a strong role in our consciousness. But the emotions you are used to feeling and the emotional patterns which you are used to - and in some cases even addicted to- also affect both thought and feeling. The core issue in addiction, for example, is recycling and being unable to let go of an emotional pattern, far more based in the old brain than managed by the new brain. Trigger the beginning emotion of an addictive cycle and you set in motion a series of emotions that lead to addictive behavior. Thinking has little to do with it. In fact, in the addictive process (and in other times in life), thinking is the slave of feelings and reasoning has little to do with the process. New findings show the old brain to be much more involved in addictive behavior than previously considered.

Our emotions are the most fundamental way that we measure our lives. We want most to "feel good". In fact, we want to feel good more than we want to "look good" because "looking good" is for the purpose of getting closer to "feeling good". In a multitude of ways, we do what we do to feel good. Our good deeds and our bad deeds are all, on some level, because we want to feel good. We may make ourselves feel bad because we think we have to feel bad to get to feeling good or to know what it's like to feel good. But feeling good doesn't depend upon feeling bad first. You will know joy because joy is joy, *not because you **had** to feel bad to know what it is*. That is a fallacy.

We want most to feel good. Even our sabotage of feeling good is, at its essence, an attempt to secure that we will feel good. It doesn't have to work that way, but often does.

Emotions are the most fundamental way we measure and describe our lives. We experience how we are by how we feel and we talk about where we are in feeling terms. Our emotions are the single most important indicator of "how we are". And it is really pretty simple: we either feel good or we feel bad. And, what's more, we know it. We always know how we feel on some level.

We ask the questions, "How am I feeling?" or "How does this make me feel?" and we know, we really know. It's much less complex than we would like to make it.

At this point you may be thinking there are people out there who really don't know and sometimes, you don't believe that you know how you're feeling. This book is for people who know what they're feeling or who can pretty much get there. It's for people who are healthy and are close to their feelings or who are tired of playing like they are victims and want to stay out of a therapist's office. This book concentrates on the far greater portion of the population that is healthy enough to know or to be pretty close to knowing what they are feeling without having to be in counseling or therapy to find out.

Granted, in some cases, all of us from time to time have difficulty knowing an immediate feeling. That's normal. You just have to be willing to leave any victim or martyr role behind and decide to "feel" your feelings, and you will do fine. A key is to recognize negative feelings and not let them be "the boss". They are just sign posts to changing your thinking and your feeling in a positive direction. Negative feelings don't own you; you can decide to feel positive feelings –if only just a little at a time.

Addicts and people with mental health issues have difficulty feeling their feelings. You can still have that problem and use the *Emotional Gym*. It's a lot like physical exercise; if you go the gym and exercise your body and continue to eat junk food, you're going to have a much harder time leaving behind those extra pounds you want to get rid of.

If you want to get into an *UpSpiral* and leave your baggage behind without having to examine it all and live like that forever, you're already motivated to do this work.

If you want to hold onto negative feelings because it feeds your sense of being a victim, this approach will not work. Negative feelings are important to people who perceive themselves as "problemed" or as victims. This work involves a conscious decision to "feel good" to feel better, to feel as good as you can possibly feel.

And you will come to realize in the process that you can have much more control over your feeling states than you ever thought possible. *You are not the victim of your emotions; you can be in charge of them.* You can have conscious control over your emotions. You can feel what you want to feel. You just have to develop the emotional muscle to do it and you have to work at it for a while. It's just like building a strong body. We do a little bit and a little bit more over time and then, one day, we realize that we feel better. In this case, it's often much faster than that. Usually, you can feel better very quickly and move to feeling good pretty rapidly. If you are filled with negative emotions and you been practicing them for a long time, it may take longer, but you can feel better, and after a time, you can – and will – actually feel good.

If you are concerned that this is a mere exercise in denial, be assured that denial is not just a negative defense mechanism; it is a positive mechanism enabling us to get on with life. Acknowledge the negative feeling. Listen to what it has to tell you about what you really want. Don't deny it, but don't be an emotional DJ and play the same emotional song all day. Instead, feel positive thoughts and positive emotions. If changing your thinking helps, then change your thinking. If it doesn't, go to a positive feeling. The exercises in this book will show you how. Changing a thought doesn't necessarily take you to a positive emotion, but changing your feelings will always change your thinking, if it is in a positive direction. Remember, this doesn't have to be an enormous leap of feeling; it is a "lean" toward the positive emotions you have been experiencing; you are telling the brain where you want to go. You are learning in the process described here to go to a positive feeling, then to be *StrengthSmart* and to go to a positive strength. When you focus on a negative thought, you only get more of it. Focus and nurture the positive and you will grow your strengths and your resilience and you will not waste your precious energy resisting.

We have a tendency to think that emotions are something that happen to us. We feel this way because of this or that outside circumstance that we see as creating this feeling state. Much of that is true because we let it be true. But it doesn't have to be true for you. The emotions you feel can be your choice. It just takes some practice. What about the past? What about our childhood? What about really bad negative experiences?

The truth is that we actually shed the skins of the past and move forward if we will allow ourselves to do so. People with high self-esteem see their past as far less significant from a negative sense than those with low self-esteem. However, interestingly enough, when people with high self-esteem experience a sustained slump in their self-esteem they lapse into finding fault and blaming difficult experiences on their pasts. Watch out, Mom! Watch out, Dad!

The better you feel, the less likely you are to see your past negatively. The worse you feel, the more hunting around in your past you are likely to do in order to find something to blame all of this on, rather than look at yourself. Look and you will find the negative and you will also find a therapist to listen to it until your insurance runs out, unless you find a good therapist who insists that you move forward with your life, in spite of your negative experiences.

What about brain chemistry? What about depression? Do you have a chemical imbalance? If so, go to a psychiatrist. Are you depressed? Then go to a psychologist or an array of professionals that treat depression. Even if you are depressed or if you have a chemical imbalance, this book can be of great help and significance. If you really want to take responsibility for how you feel, the *Emotional Gym* and the focus of this book will enable you to do just that.

When you go to a gym, you go to take responsibility for your body. You go to work out, become physically stronger and to improve your overall health and fitness. The *Emotional Gym* is no different; you go to this gym and do an emotional work out, to tone and shape your emotional life to do the things you need to do. You go to this gym to "feel good". If you make the decision that you want to "feel good" and you begin to believe - as you incorporate the material in this book - that you can, you will. You will! There is a strong cultural bias when it comes to feelings. We tend

The better you feel, the less likely you are to see your past negatively. The worse you feel, the more hunting around in your past you are likely to do in order to find something to blame all of this on, rather than look at yourself.

to believe that negative feelings always have to be aired or talked out or solved. We tend to believe that there is a negative energy in negative feelings that if not aired or released will always double back on us as repressed conflict. One more time, the truth is that we shed the skins of the past if, and this is an important *if*, we are moving forward, growing, learning, developing and exercising our strengths. There is a normal process of living that undoes the negative, without our focusing on the negative and having to talk everything out or dwell on it. We are overly "counseled" and "therapized" in this culture, with the idea that the only model for resolving conflict or negativity is to focus on it, to shine a light on it, to bring it to the surface, to work it out, to resolve it. Sometimes that may be the case, but most of the time it is the normal process of living and growing that makes us bigger and better and enables us to simply leave most negativity behind us. The truth is, often we just don't want to let go of the negative and get on with our lives. We would rather nurse our wounds, or hold onto them as a possible future escape hatch, instead of facing the challenges of living fully alive focusing on our strengths and our potential.

Isn't this denial, you may continue to wonder? Won't that cause repression, you may be asking? The answer to both is yes, it may be denial and it may be repression, but neither of these defenses is negative in nature. They've just gotten a bad one-sided "rap". They are good things –in fact, they are some of the things that help us get on with our lives. However, as we grow, whatever we do need to "open us" or "heal" or "talk out" comes up at the right time if it's a significant block for us and most of the time it's not, if we are growing and moving ahead with our lives.

When my son played baseball, I would go to his games after a day of doing therapy and one day I was struck between the eyes by something the astute coach of these little boys was doing. Every time they missed the ball, every time they struck and missed and every single time they struck out, he would yell "shake it off", "Shake it off Danny", "Shake it off, Eddie", Shake it off Joel". SHAKE IT OFF. Sometimes the boys would literally, between the pitch of the ball, take their hands and "shake it off". It was a wonderful lesson to watch. This coach knew that if these kids were going to hit the next ball, he didn't have time for a special conference or even a pat on the back; they would just have to "shake it off" if they were going to hit the next pitch or be ready to hit again at their next time up to bat if they struck out the last time. Shake it off. What good advice in an overly pandered to, in search of every morsel of approval, lick our wounds, overly sensitive culture of political correctness. "Shake it off" is good advice on many levels. Shake it off and pay attention to the next pitch or you going to lose the game.

I was painfully aware of having an office often filled with people who wouldn't shake off the last strike and were missing the next pitch in the game of their life, so much so that they were either losing or had given up playing with little determination. *Shake it off and play ball.*

Far too much time is spent in counseling and therapy offices digging for issues that need no immediate attention if they ever needed any at all. Shine the light on what is negative and wrong and that's what you're going to grow. What you focus on is what you get. If negative experiences are causing significant difficulties in getting on with your life, they will present themselves at "the right time" in a way that they can be aired, while, at the same time, you are choosing to plan and take the next steps in positive growth. Too often everyday problems are diagnosed by poorly skilled

> Counseling and therapy can spend way too much time digging, and much more needless time seeing "what comes up". If it isn't pressing against forward making progress – really pressing – then leave it alone and move on.

professionals who need to fill their practices. To do so, they utilize **DSM V**, the manual of mental disorders, to create something like an "anxiety disorder". It would be revealing to know how many people who never needed to be in counseling or therapy have received this diagnosis, and enter into a system of labeling and belief that have kept them there, identifying each as a victim far longer than they needed, if they ever had a need. The diagnostic criteria of excessive worry or anxiety for a six month period can be made to fit almost anybody, and can therefore cover most anything. Once given a diagnostic number (300.02 for generalized anxiety disorder) for diagnostic purposes, that number also enables third party insurance payment. When insurance companies began to limit the amount of therapy to a certain number of sessions, "short-term psychotherapy" came into vogue. Anyone who thinks that they are protected by confidentiality is wrong. This diagnostic number remains on your record forever; it never gets removed because you recover, get better and leave it behind. And while the therapist is bound by laws of confidentiality, there are job applications that require the release of all medical information to be considered for employment. The implications of entry into the mental health system are considerable and ought not to be overlooked.

Counseling and therapy can spend way too much time digging, and much more needless time seeing "what comes up". If it isn't pressing against forward making progress – really pressing – then leave it alone and move on. Keep your eye on the next pitch of life so you can hit or move out of its way if the ball might hit you. You can't get on base if you aren't swinging at the ball and you can't swing at the ball if you're in some dug-out talking to a therapist about the game you're missing.

Resilience and bouncing back is all about what you decide to make of any negative situation and what you're going to do with it. The faster you move on to a positive emotion, the better off you are. The inclination of our times is to think that talking about every negative thing that ever happened to you to a therapist is often not about resilience and healing, but is rather about creating victims. These 'victims' talk about their negative issues far too long without making significant plans to "feel better" and to "feel good". We are a nation of people psychologized into being "victims", talking about the game, rather than actively playing it, and then resenting the fact that we aren't.

We give much too much attention to what is wrong rather than what is right, We focus much too much light on problems and negative feelings and not nearly enough with getting on with it. We are made to be resilient and to "bounce back". And the process of healing depends on the forward moving process of growth to bring strength, resilience and "bounce back".

The *Emotional Gym* is about getting on with it, about your capacity to feel positive feelings and to build strong emotional muscle into your life without dwelling on every negative event and emotion that has occurred in your life.

The forward moving process of growth will do its own healing as

> Resilience and bouncing back is all about what you decide to make of any negative situation and what you're going to do with it. The faster you move on to a positive emotion, the better off you are.

long as you let it. This book is about that process. There are plenty of other authors with thousands of pages written about healing. The *Emotional Gym* is about wellness and about moving on with your life. But you have to be willing to take your focus off of the "condition", off the problem and put it on the solution.

In this process you're going to learn to focus on positive emotions and to forget about the negative ones for a while. And after a while, you will forget about most of them. Those you don't forget and you still want to talk through, can be handled later. When you grow stronger and more confident and when you "feel good", not a lot of time gets spent on talking about what "feels bad" because it just doesn't seem that important. It doesn't fit the ongoing flow of life. Talking about the negative will feel against the flow of the positive stride of life.

Ask yourself this simple question. Would you rather talk about your negative feelings and focus and grow more negative feelings or would you rather feel good? If you believe that talking about negative feelings, always "airing" your problems and complaints relieves them, you're wrong. You're just flat out, wrong. For a while, their energy seems to be gone, but if you have not turned from that and done something else more positive in the meantime, they will return, and you know it. You've been there, done that! You know they return and need to be aired again and again, until you "decide" to stop talking about them. You can spend as much time as you want talking about your negative feelings, but the more time you spend doing so, the greater portion of your life you will spend in what becomes a very unproductive and dangerous habit. You will have spent a lot of time in the "dug out" and waste a lot of your psychic energy. Move on.

The *Emotional Gym* is about feeling positive emotion as a *cause rather than an effect. We are going to use positive emotion first as the cause and let it create its effect.* Many of us think that the only time we can experience positive emotion is if there is an obvious reason. Some "thing" or some "one" makes us happy. Some event makes us joyful. Something causes us to experience a positive emotion. The problem here is that you can wait a long time until the positive event comes along, too long - way, way, too long sometimes. You can make yourself feel what you want to feel.

We need to experience, grow, build and develop positive emotions every day. Our brains need it, our bodies need it, and our cells need positive emotion to thrive. Positive emotion has got to be a part of our diet of experience everyday. We get it by feeling it and we feel it by choice.

What you are going to learn to do is to breathe oxygen to the centers of the brain where positive emotion is stored. And by exercising these positive emotional centers in the brain, you will be building psychological capital by increasing the inter-neuronal association in the brain. Positive emotions "open" the brain or increase receptivity across the brain by increasing brain synchronicity and rhythm. Positive emotions are, for the brain, a kind of lubricant leading to easier flow of information and the association of that information in various kinds of memory and "knowing" throughout and across the brain. I would go so far as to say that positive emotions are the lubricant of the neuroplasticity of the brain.

Neuroplasticity is the capacity of the brain to re-wire itself, to establish new circuits of neuronal transmission. The simpler way of saying this is that your brain's neurons will be able to talk positively to each other to a much greater extent throughout your brain. The channels of positivity in your brain will increase in three significant ways: immediacy, duration and intensity. These are the three ways we measure and work with emotions. Immediacy refers to how you can access the emotion instantly. Duration is the "staying power" of how to get an emotion to last over a period of time. And finally, intensity is the capacity to increase, at will, the amplitude or level of an emotion. You can learn to do all three at will and at anytime in any situation. Doing so can transform not only how you feel, but how you think and how you behave. You will learn how to do it here.

As you get more and more used to practicing accessing positive

> Positive emotions are, for the brain, a kind of lubricant leading to easier flow of information and the association of that information in various kinds of memory and "knowing" throughout and across the brain.

emotions, as you build this energy that we are calling psychological capital, you are also building a "buffer zone" of positivity. This buffer zone protects against what is negative and creates a resistance to disease and a greater immunology to what seems negative in life. In other words, it will take longer for things to get to you and to affect you in a negative way. What does affect you negatively will have a shorter life. In this work we are always moving the "lean" of the brain, its directionality, toward a positive state of feeling and perceiving. It is actually incorrect to say that you are "moving" anything; this is already the natural "lean" of the brain. You are cooperating and enhancing that natural tendency of your brain and its evolution. You are creating nothing less than the *rudiments* of State of Mind Management (SOMM). It is the beginning of the management of mood. You cannot manage mood without gaining greater conscious control of your feelings.

Negative feelings are guideposts. They tell you to move toward the positive. It is not that you ignore negative feelings. They just tell you to go in the other direction. They don't need to be analyzed, dissected, labeled, or quantified. They need to be left behind as quickly as possible. Most of the time they are telling you to move in the other direction, toward what feels good. Even in trauma – in fact, especially in trauma. The fastest way out of trauma is to move in a positive direction and to quarantine negative emotions and deal with them at the appropriate time and from a positive state of mind. Swim out of danger into soft and soothing waters of what is positive and good. When people say "I don't want to think about it," "I don't want to talk about it," they mean it. They really don't want to talk or think about it, for good reason! Stop hovering like a vulture feeding on what is dying, and let people move into the light and into the fresh air and leave behind what they want to leave behind without labeling this healthy denial and repression as a negative.

People know when they are ready to talk about something, if, in fact, that is the way they process negative emotion at all. Negativity is processed in a hundred creative, life-giving, life healing ways, and in the time-space the individual finds comfortable for them. This is true for everyone, but it is most especially true with children. Too many therapists are simply disguised negative emotional voyeurs; watch out for them and watch who you share your negative feelings with. Let it be with people who move out of them and into the positive as quickly as possible.

Ready for a work-out in the *Emotional Gym?*

Let's start with one "lead" emotion and then add three others to that. The lead emotion is gratitude. Gratitude is the "default setting" of your emotional range. Gratitude is one of the top "strengths" of happy people. When in doubt, go to gratitude. Whenever you have spare time, immerse yourself in gratitude. Whenever your brain is wandering, experience gratitude. When you're in traffic, go to gratitude. When you hear a great song, go to gratitude. In fact, even when you hear a lousy song, go to gratitude. Get it?

Always go to the feeling of gratitude, and work at making it become the state of mind to which you are most accustomed and in which you are most comfortable. This is the first step in SOMM. SOMM is the development, over time, of this predisposition to "lean" or gravitate toward certain mood states or states of mind. You are working toward something like a "default setting". You just go there. You'll get used to being there; you'll become accustomed to going there. All it takes is persistence and practice. For example, I have a client who has practiced himself into easily going to anger or frustration. We "practice" him toward peace. You can practice yourself toward a state of mind by, over a period of time, feeling these other emotions. To state it again, the emotions we feel are not necessarily the result of thoughts or patterns of thought. Emotions are much more basal than how we normally describe thinking.

The first exercise in the *Emotional Gym* chapter will move you in that direction. It is a decision to use gratitude as a lead and key emotion that you want to train your self to feel. It is the closest alternate route, when done in gradients, to get to a positive state of mind. There are enormous benefits to feeling gratitude and being in a state of mind of gratitude. The body chemistry associated with gratitude is the most optimally healthy state of mind. There is scientific evidence showing that a positive state of mind affects thriving at a cellular level. Research conducted by pioneers like Candice Pert and Bruce Lipton identifies an intricate relationship between our beliefs and attitudes (our feeling states) to the process of cellular life that includes the elimination and assimilation activity of healthy thriving cells.

You may be thinking, "What about the times when I just can't feel grateful –it just won't come, it just isn't there." Don't start there,

> It is a decision to use gratitude as a lead and key emotion that you want to train your self to feel. It is the closest alternate route, when done in gradients, to get to a positive state of mind.

and don't worry about those times. Start with when you get up in the morning or start when your mind wanders. Start with the spaces of your day when you could just as easily go to gratitude as thinking about the weather. Start going to gratitude a hundred little times a day and it will begin to affect the times that gratitude is difficult. Dan Gilbert, in his research on happiness, shows us that a hundred smaller hits of happiness are more important than larger and more significant ones over a period of time. And after a while, gratitude will not be difficult to find. It can be accessed and felt more and more quickly and easily. You best practice a positive state of mind by making it more pervasive when you are feeling it. Let it extend to everything; let it color everything and make it last longer. This is the dimension of "duration" in measuring the strengths of an emotion.

Here is a promise that will help. The more time you spend in a state of mind of gratitude, the more you are going to find that you get what you want in life. Gratitude will make you more effective, more creative, and more receptive to the good things in life. It is a part of the first PROMISE of this book, Get into a state of mind of gratitude on a daily basis, live from this emotional setting, by your own choice, and you'll get more of what you want out of life. *It's a promise.*

To start your workout in the *Emotional Gym*, each day feel the feeling of gratitude ten times in rapid succession. On a scale of 1-10 if 10 is as much gratitude as you could possibly ever feel, feel just a 1 or 2 - just a little gratitude. In the beginning, you can't make great jumps of emotion quickly. It takes practice. Even as you improve, it is still good to feel more emotion a little at a time, although later on you'll find yourself able to make bigger jumps. If you went to a gym to build your physical muscle, you wouldn't start with the heaviest weight; you'd start with a lighter one that was comfortable for you. Do the same here; start easy. Close your eyes and feel gratitude at a 1 or 2 on this scale, for 10-20 seconds. Then let it go, and feel it again. If you can feel the feeling outright, that's great, but if not, then just think of something that you are grateful for. It can be anything as simple as the fact that your heart is beating, you are breathing, or that your bowels moved today (you'd be very unhappy in a day or two if that didn't happen, so be grateful it did). Feel the feeling of gratitude for just a few seconds and then let it go and return to it. You are doing a kind of pulsing of the feeling.

What you are doing is sending a signal to the neurons in your brain, where gratitude is stored. You are turning this center on and are breathing oxygen into it and waking it up. The best part is, you are doing it "at will" and "on call", by your choice. You are establishing "immediate" recall,, an important measure of conscious control of an emotional state. Having immediate emotional access to these emotions is a positive thing, and you get it through practice and exercise. Imagine that as you do this, there is actually gratitude spreading across your brain. You are making your brain smile. And gratitude can spread in the brain like wildfire -----whoosh, the brain loves gratitude. *It's like giving your brain a massage.*

Do this every day for a month - no days off. With this exercise, your brain best understands constancy and persistence. It will take only a few minutes, three or four at the most, but they are precious moments. You will be instructing the plasticity of your brain to do something new and it will take it a while to get this new order down and in place. We will build other exercises on top of this in every chapter, but this is where the *Emotional Gym* starts. It takes a small amount of time everyday, just a minute or two to wake your brain up to the new choice that you are going to go to gratitude, "on call", by your own choice.

After practicing ten repetitions of gratitude, do the same thing with love, joy, peace, and hope. You will be lifting the five emotional weights as you start your *Emotional Gym* workout: gratitude, love, joy, peace, and hope. In total, you do not need to spend more than three or four minutes and you can choose your own order. Likely, one or more of these emotions will be difficult for you. Just feel what you can for now. As you progress, you will feel more over time. These four emotions are the most significant for brain synchronicity, conservation of psychic energy and evolution to higher states of consciousness and even the elasticity and growth of intelligence.

There may be an emotion that gives you great difficulty to feel - perhaps love. If you can't feel love, then feel gratitude instead. Gratitude will eventually open up access to all of the emotions. Feel gratitude until you can get to love.

For the most part, you will start off feeling a small part of all of these positive emotions. If you can't, don't worry. Instead, focus on what you can do.

The important thing is to start working toward feeling positive emotion and getting to these positive emotions with *immediacy.*

Let's review just what you are doing here. You are not waiting for a "cause" to feel positive emotion. *You are making the emotion the cause itself, and you are causing yourself to feel the emotion.* You are building the first of three dimensions of an emotion: immediacy. In later chapters, you will be building duration (holding the emotion over a period of time) and intensity (increasing the emotion over a period of time).

This is the beginning of SOMM. You can have conscious control over your feeling states; you do not have to be the victim of your emotions any longer.

Workout #1: The *Emotional Gym*

1. Make a decision to start the *Emotional Gym* and embrace and incorporate it every day for thirty days.

2. Feel the emotions of gratitude, love, joy, peace, and hope 10 times a day. On a scale of 1-10, if 1 is a little and 10 is a lot, feel the emotions at a 3 or a 4. Feel each emotion for about 5-10 seconds each time. You are *"pulsing"* the emotion 10 times at a low level of feeling. Don't try to make the emotion last longer and don't try to make it more intense. Work for a series of ten pulses of gratitude for Then do the same thing with the other primary emotions of love, peace, joy, and hope. The purpose is to learn to get to the feeling of "gratitude" instantly, on call.

This is our first measure of the strength of an emotion. Why? This is a powerful exercise of conditioning for the brain. It begins to train the brain to feel "a little" of the emotion and you begin to develop regulation of the emotion. You are after a kind of chronic, low grade, consistent emotion of gratitude, then love, then joy, then peace, and then hope. If you can't feel one of the emotions, then just think them and you will get there. *It is better to feel an emotion consistently, in working out at your Emotional Gym, at a low level than to feel the emotion only periodically at a higher level.* So work at achieving this low level of emotion. Do the exercise as often as you think of it, over and over again during the day. Whenever you are standing in a line, waiting, or doing anything repetitive or mindless, use these times to train your brain toward a default setting that is positive.

You are beginning to grow a positive mind. If you already have a positive mind, you are making it stronger. It is this positive mind that will get you into an *UpSpiral*. The energy and natural velocity of The *UpSpiral* will take you higher in the positive mind, but the *Emotional Gym* will be a constant source of strengthening to keep you there.

The *UpSpiral* is the next chapter here and in your life. Go there full of anticipation. It is full of the unfolding promises of the positive mind.

Emotional Gym Summary

Because we tend to think that emotions just happen to us, it is not always apparent to us that we create our emotions, and that we can utilize, direct, and control our emotional states and moods.

An increased bank account or reserve (a buffer) of positive emotions will make you more resistant to negative emotions. This reservoir of practiced emotion will reduce the "staying power" of negative emotions. Build your reservoir and you will get rid of negative emotions more quickly.

The better you feel, the less likely you are to see your past negatively. The worse you feel, the more hunting around in your past you are likely to do in order to find something to blame all of this on, rather than look at yourself.

Counseling and therapy can spend way too much time digging, and much more needless time seeing "what comes up". If it isn't pressing against forward making progress – really pressing – then leave it alone and move on.

Resilience and bouncing back is all about what you decide to make of any negative situation and what you're going to do with it. The faster you move on to a positive emotion, the better off you are.

Positive emotions are, for the brain, a kind of lubricant leading to easier flow of information and the association of that information in various kinds of memory and "knowing" throughout and across the brain.

It is a decision to use gratitude as a lead and key emotion that you want to train your self to feel. It is the closest alternate route, when done in gradients, to get to a positive state of mind.

The UpSpiral

You can stay in an *UpSpiral* 100% of the time and by being there raise both your happiness and your emotional set-points and "feel good" most all of the time.

To grow a positive mind from which you become who you really are and from which you attract into your life what you really want, you have to learn how to stay in an *UpSpiral*. Nothing anyone wants can be found in a *DownSpiral*.

You may have to get into a *DownSpiral* in order to look up and know that it's not where you want to be, but it isn't necessary to do that. You have heard that what goes up must come down. The *UpSpiral* defies that notion; in your *UpSpiral*, what goes up is a part of a spiral of energy and stability and mood and what goes up can go up and can remain there and can even go higher.

To grow a positive mind from which you become who you really are and from which you attract into your life what you really want, you have to learn how to stay in an *UpSpiral*. Nothing anyone wants can be found in a *DownSpiral*.

The *UpSpiral* is very simply this: it is "feeling good".

The *UpSpiral* is a spiral of positive emotion and energy and you can be in that spiral 100% of the time. The *UpSpiral* is a spiral that is a positive frame of mind, a state of mind that sees things from a positive perspective. It has been described as optimism, but it is more than that; it is an energy that is also a flow that builds psychological capital. It is a combination of energy, positive emotion, and faith, a sense of self and personal meaning. Psychological capital is something like resilience. It is the capacity to feel good at a marked level for a long period of time. It is the capacity to raise your emotional and happiness set-point.

We once thought that your emotional and happiness set points, were, in fact, set, as in "genetically inherited". We now know that they are not set. They may be genetically influenced or predisposed, but they are anything but set. You can increase both your level of happiness and your positive emotional state and make it last.

This builds to sustain itself and acts as a buffer against disease and negative experiences. There will be more about psychological capital and "the buffer zone" later. For now, let's focus in on positive emotion.

> The *UpSpiral* is a spiral of positive emotion and energy and you can be in that spiral 100% of the time. The *UpSpiral* is a spiral that is a positive frame of mind, a state of mind that sees things from a positive perspective. It has been described as optimism, but it is more than that; it is an energy that is also a flow that builds psychological capital.

Until recent empirical research was undertaken, positive emotion had not gotten much good press. Positive emotion has been seen as a luxury or as something to be stumbled upon if you're lucky. Even with such notable figures as Norman Cousins and his classic book,

Anatomy of an Illness, positive emotion still has a tough time of it. We tend to see positive emotion, while desirable, as both unattainable over a long period of time and not really a very realistic state of mind. We are suspicious of positive emotion, if not almost fearful of it. We believe that positive emotion or feeling good or a positive state of mind is something that happens to us rather than something we create. To the contrary, a positive mind is something you grow. We even tend to see positive emotion as unenlightened and see negative emotion and even cynicism as more intellectual or the result of being more keenly analytical. Nothing could be more wrong. Jim Collins in **Good to Great** notes that the Disney Empire was built on an "aim" or direction that specifically included an abhorrence of cynicism.

Our popular notion of being positive is still viewed pretty much as a "**Pollyanna**" notion rather than what "reality" really is. I decided to go back and watch Disney Studios, **Pollyanna**, in preparing for writing this book. I wanted to see why the term is used so freely to label and diminish the significance of positive emotion.

When I watched **Pollyanna** again after many years, I found the movie to be simple and profound. **Pollyanna** went around her village playing a game called the "glad game". She looked at every situation and tried to find what there was to be "glad" about. That it could be so simple or even possible is really rather scary. Certainly intellectual, sophisticated people don't go around looking for things to be "glad" about. I recommend this Disney movie highly for both mental health and well-being. But it's so simple, that I need to make it more complex so you'll "buy" it. Life's greatest gifts often make their initial appearance disguised as problems. Even in situations where there seems to be no "glad", our first creative impulse needs to be, "What creative good can come from this?" And by asking the question, sincere in the pursuit, the Universe will yield bountiful solutions and answers. Simply by asking the question, consciousness is shifted from "powerlessness" to the empowerment of the journey of seeking to create.

The second thing that **Pollyanna** pointed out to a raving fundamentalist minister in her village was that there were over 800 positive admonitions to "be glad and rejoice" in the Bible. The minister counted them and assured his congregants that there were exactly 826. **Pollyanna** told him that it was in the Bible so many times so people wouldn't forget. I heard from another source that there are four times as many mentions of "gladness and rejoicing" as there are mentions of "sin".

Pessimism is an overwhelming factor in health-related issues and in personal success and achievement. It really is our number one health problem and the greatest deterrent of well-being and life satisfaction.

Why is it that we are much more tuned into sin than into being glad and rejoicing? The Russian scientist, Zeigarnik, found from her research (which was funded by the dictator Stalin, and done under his regime) that we are nine times more likely to remember or to focus on something negative than something positive. You might think that those are odds that are hard to reverse. But that's not true. These odds can be reversed and you can do it. Positive emotion is stronger and has more energy and influence than negative emotion. Even though we may be conditioned by evolution and culture to be inclined to focus on the negative, the brain is designed to move to the positive; that is the way it evolves and regenerates itself. The nature of the energy of the brain or the "disposition" of the brain is toward what is positive and life-giving. The brain always seeks to move from conflict to synchronicity and to rhythms that most effectively use psychic energy. Sleep is the function of the brain reestablishing its equilibrium. It is psychic conflict, not physical exertion, which is most taxing on the brain and requires the greatest need for rest and sleep. Physical exhaustion takes second place to the toll of psychic conflict, which upsets the synchronicity and vibrations of the brain.

What is cultural does not have be your truth. You can reverse it. Your brain will cooperate because that is where your brain wants to go. The exercises in this book and the *Emotional Gym* will go far in restoring the positive state that is optimum for the health and functioning of your brain.

These "**Pollyanna**" lessons are significant. But our use of the term "**Pollyanna**" that has proceeded from these lessons is even more interesting. Because of the Zeigarnik effect, we have diminished this notion of positive thinking, to play it down in favor of a more critical, careful, pessimistically derived, view of things. What has seemed safer and wiser, which is to be more pessimistic, is in fact, more lethal. The research by Dr. Martin Seligman on pessimism and its effects on health are more than sobering. The effects of pessimism on success, accomplishment and achievement are equally concerning. Pessimism is an overwhelming factor in health-related issues and in personal success and achievement. It really is our number one health problem and the greatest deterrent of well-being and life satisfaction.

So where is the proof of the importance of positive emotion? There is, in fact, more and more proof. Dr. Barbara Fredrickson at the University of North Carolina at Chapel Hill won the Templeton prize in religion for her outstanding research on positive emotion. It is this research that has been a key resource underpinning the development of the new positive psychology.

Fredrickson asks the question, "What is the purpose of positive emotion?" In regards to evolution, it has stayed with us; what is its purpose? If we have survived by "fight" or "flight" and gotten to where we are, why do we have positive emotions? As it turns out, positive emotions are coming to be seen as even more important than "fight or flight", *especially in this period of our evolutionary history*, which signals a paradigm shift in the nature of evolution in this new millennium.

Fredrickson's research points to at least six things that are the result of positive emotions.

1. We learn faster.
2. We are more creative.
3. We are better at problem solving.
4. We score higher on every test of well-being when we are in an *UpSpiral* of positive emotion.
5. We score higher on every test of life-satisfaction when we are in an *UpSpiral*.
6. We thrive physically and at a cellular level.

Fredrickson expounds a theory called "Broaden and Build". Her research shows, when we are in an upward spiral we have increased access to a much broader repertoire of our thoughts and feelings. As we think from the range of this repertoire accessible in our brains, we build upon it and it broadens. Negative feeling or emotions do the opposite; it narrows us by narrowing our access to our own sense of variety and choice. Consequently, we feel like we have fewer or no choices and we feel trapped.

From positive emotions or from the *UpSpiral*, there is a greater inter-association of the neurons in the brain. Think of your brain talking to itself and all of its different parts and making connections, more and more and more all the time. In fact; a vast number of connections that we will call psychological capital are made, which also impacts the *neuroplasticity* of the brain. Neuroplasticity is the ability of the brain to grow new pathways, not only for physical movement or memory functions, but new ways of knowing and being that constitute a higher degree of human consciousness. It is the ability of your brain to rewire and reprogram itself. The growing and building of positive emotion creates an *UpSpiral*.

Here are some of the profound implications of the *UpSpiral*. The growing and building of positive emotion creates an *UpSpiral*. It is a spiral that grows and increases, in and of itself, once it has begun. Positive emotions grow positive actions and positive moods, states of mind, and positive actions create more positive emotions.

> Neuroplasticity is the ability of the brain to grow new pathways, not only for physical movement or memory functions, but new ways of knowing and being that constitute a higher degree of human consciousness. It is the ability of your brain to rewire and reprogram itself. The growing and building of positive emotion creates an *UpSpiral*.

In your desire to grow a more positive mind, you are actually doing that growing. Your mind has an enormous capacity to program the growth, the structure and the nature of your brain. We already know that the brain has this capacity to be highly malleable. Your brain will wander if you let it wander, it will unfold if we just want life to "to unfold" or, it will grow in a positive direction that enlarges your strengths, sheds the skin of the negativity of the past, and increases not only your creativity and your intelligence, but also your joy and your capacity to "feel good". And it will do so all of your life until you die.

What about the declining, aging brain? The brain ages, but, like fine wine, it does not have to decline. The brain develops throughout all of life. There does not have to be a decline. Rather, the brain, as a developmental task in the second half of life, transfers the psychic energy of things like short-term memory into things like "getting the larger picture" so that life will be lived on a plane of wider and fuller satisfaction. This paradox of the brain aging, over and against the fact that it also is engaged is getting the "larger picture" is precisely among the issues addressed in Goldberg's **The Wisdom Paradox.** For a much more extensive discussion of these issues read this provocative analysis.

Let's take a minute here and look at this more closely. After about

> The brain ages, but, like fine wine, does not have to decline. The brain develops throughout all of life. There does not have to be a decline. Rather, the brain, as a developmental task in the second half of life, transfers the psychic energy of things like short-term memory into things like "getting the larger picture" so that life will be lived on a plane of wider and fuller satisfaction.

age 15 or 17, the right hemisphere of the brain, which has been, up to that point, almost totally in charge of learning a language, refuses to do so any longer. Then, learning a language becomes a whole brain activity and much less automatic. So, we know that the brain can change in function and structure. This is also true with short-term memory. Your brain is not going to cooperate in remembering every name, every face, where you put your keys, or every phone number. It just isn't going to cooperate with "diddle" in the second half of life. It has a bigger developmental job and that is to get you to do "large term, wide range thinking" so you can get the bigger picture. Why? So you can be wiser, happier and more content. The brain likes to be positive and happy. Who lives the longest? Astronomers. Why not, they spend all of their time looking at the bigger picture. You do the same and you will likely live longer with a healthier brain. In the meantime, don't buy into the drug companies that are inventing pills to save your short-term memory; your brain doesn't want to go there. The master design is greater consciousness and wisdom.

As the brain becomes more positive, we become more intelligent, diverse and creative in our thinking. By the nature of the more positive life we are living, we attract to us more of the things we want because we are living in the direction of getting what is important to us. We also become healthier at a cellular level. Cells thrive, which means that the balance of the cells is in greater harmony. Our cells are eliminating what is not needed and assimilating what is needed for healthy growth. Upset this balance and you interrupt thriving at a cellular level and the disease process can begin. In **The Biology of Belief**, Bruce Lipton explains his research that it is our beliefs that most influence our thriving at a cellular level.

In this process of the association of neurons across the brain, the neurons are doing something like wrapping themselves, insulating themselves against disease. Your brain will become more resistant to Alzheimer's and dementia.

Consider the opposite of the *UpSpiral*: the *DownSpiral*. We all know how rapidly we can get into a downward spiral by entertaining negative thoughts or by being in negative situations that lower our positive vibration. The *DownSpiral* narrows our access to our repertoire of thinking and knowledge. We are less able to make good choices because we aren't in a creative place to think about these choices. In the *DownSpiral* we can see only what's wrong, only what's not good. We see more narrowly and we certainly can't see the big picture, only what's wrong with parts of it.

Consider for a moment that you are on the NASA team. Your job is to look for things that could go wrong and to report them. Remember those people on the NASA team who were supposed to report the tiles on the side of the space ship that weren't functioning? It's not that they didn't notice the problem. But in a culture, largely colored by *DownSpiral* thinking, they didn't report it. It doesn't take a *DownSpiral* to exercise the strengths that notice what is wrong and correct it; it takes an *UpSpiral* and the exercise of critical strengths that will take positive action. Long scrutinizing studies and investigations were conducted to identify that, indeed, NASA had changed from a culture of the *UpSpiral* to one of the *DownSpiral*, where creativity, positivity, and openness were not encouraged. The same work culture that produces real creativity and growth is the same work culture that produces great scrutiny and fearlessness in identifying and addressing problems head on. These work cultures know that problems are opportunities for growth in disguise.

There are those who say the downward spiral and pessimism have a value for us, and we need, at times, to think more critically by being in a *DownSpiral*. There has been some research to attempt to prove this is true.

However, I would conclude that the research is extremely limited because it looked at the nature of critical thinking only from the perspective that pessimism is essentially necessary for critical thinking. It is not. The crucial part of the research that is missing concerns the development of strengths exercised from an *UpSpiral* and employed to do the same critical thinking. You don't have to be pessimistic to think critically. You have to use your strengths and play to your strengths in the *UpSpiral* and you will think more critically, more creatively, and you will be far more likely to take critical and decisive action without fear of retribution. These strengths will be talked about in the next chapter, *StrengthSmart*.

The *UpSpiral* is not just a good idea; it should be the way of life you choose. You have the choice. Life needs to be lived in the *UpSpiral* and none of life needs to be lived in a *DownSpiral*. This is likely one of the most important discoveries of the new millennium. All of our lives can be in an *UpSpiral*, including the pain and difficulty of life. If we can learn how to maintain an *UpSpiral* in difficult times, these difficult times can show us the difference between pain and suffering. Perhaps we don't have to suffer nearly as much as we thought. Perhaps it is not true that we have to dig ourselves into a hole before we can have a turn around and be successful. Perhaps it is not true that to really feel good, we have to feel bad. In fact, it isn't true. You don't have to fail before you can succeed. And when you succeed you don't have to sabotage that success to learn the important lessons in life. You also do not have to sabotage "easy" success because it should have required more "struggle", more toil, more anguish and more sweat. Perhaps your greatest struggle is just to relish your success.

We have justified much of our suffering because we want to make

You don't have to be pessimistic to think critically. You have to use your strengths and play to your strengths in the *UpSpiral* and you will think more critically, more creatively, and you will be far more likely to take critical and decisive action without fear of retribution. These strengths will be talked about in the next chapter, *StrengthSmart*.

it a "necessary" part of our learning. What if all of this suffering isn't as necessary as we seem to think that it is? Certainly we learn from our mistakes. They are gifts, without question. But we need to get past the paradigm of "death to life" and struggle to success. It doesn't have to be like that for everybody. It is entirely possible to sing a beautiful love song without having had three miserable relationships. The experience of the opposite does not necessarily determine that we will be able to better experience the other. You can go to joy and stay there, with out experiencing sadness. Our lives, as they are, give us enough contrast to know what we want, without having to experience a greater misery to know that we want to feel good. *We believe too much in the essential nature of opposites. The delicate shades and experiences of our lives are enough to move us to what we want, if we believe they are. All of the drama just isn't essential unless we believe that it is.*

There are many people who have been more or less happy and content all of their lives. They have known joy and their lives have not been marked by severe ups and downs or a great deal of suffering. They are still capable of deep feelings, their lives are still rich, and they aren't at all superficial. We just haven't paid much attention to them and they have remained "unglorified" in part because many tend to believe that there must be suffering and drama for their lives to be of enormous significance. Many who judge their lives to be rather ordinary and uneventful remain in a kind of hiding. But they are there, many of them, with happy lives who defy this standard that the depth of life can only be experienced if you have suffered deeply. *While learning through suffering cannot be discounted, it is only one way, and is far over –rated and much of it is unnecessary and unproductive in producing the deep results we would like to believe it portends.*

Learning to live in an *UpSpiral* will make our lives easier, more pleasant, more fun, and more exciting. We can live in an UpSpiral much more of the time than we might have thought possible. We can live in an *UpSpiral* much more of the time. It is a matter of choice. An excellent resource in this area is written by the former Under Secretary to U Thant at the United Nations. Robert Mueller, who survived Nazi incarceration and the war, writes about this *UpSpiral* and how he achieved it all of his life in a book called, **Most of All They Taught Me Happiness**.

The first goal for the clients I work with is for them to grow to a point of being in an *UpSpiral* 95% of the time. My clients have shown me that they can be there 100% of the time. They know that it is even possible to go through the toughest times in life and remain in an *UpSpiral* of hope and confidence. It is a decision. Once the decision to live in the *UpSpiral* is made it takes practice and intentionality, but once you pass though this door and experience prolonged periods of being in the *UpSpiral*, you will simply not want to turn around and go back to where you were. You will be much more sensitive to what no longer "fits" and you won't want to go there. You'll be in a new place, so new that you can't, in fact, go back. There is no turning around once you have experienced life in the *UpSpiral*.

StrengthSmart – A Way to Stay in the *UpSpiral*

Our lives, as they are, give us enough contrast to know what we want, without having to experience a greater misery to know that we want to feel good. *We believe too much in the essential nature of opposites. The delicate shades and experiences of our lives are enough to move us to what we want, if we believe they are. All of the drama just isn't essential unless we believe that it is.*

In the next chapter, you will learn the importance of the strengths that are uniquely yours. You will be guided to take two tests to show you what those strengths are. When you finish with the tests, you will know that your top 10 strengths work most for you in your growth and that they are primary tools you use to stay in an *UpSpiral*.

When you are in an *UpSpiral* there is a 9 to 1 chance that you will be more likely to use your strengths if you know what they are and have become reflexive in using them. In fact, people who spend more of their time in an *UpSpiral* intuitively know and play to their strengths. People in a *DownSpiral* play to their weaknesses. Your weaknesses are simply the opposite side of your strengths. In other words, they are two ends of the same stick. Generally when you "feel good" you play to your strengths and when you "feel bad" you play to your weaknesses.

Staying in an *UpSpiral* is, then, a determining factor in using your strengths in everyday life and, in turn, using your strengths will help to maintain you in an *UpSpiral*. *StrengthSmart* will teach you how to do this.

Let's talk about health-related issues. There are several resources in the back of the book that deal with health issues. But here is a central consideration. People who spend their time in the *DownSpiral* are twice as likely to have a stroke or heart attack. If you get nothing more from this book than understanding this fact, it will have been worth my effort as the author and your effort as the reader. You could save your life and major health consequences by staying in an *UpSpiral*. It is the *DownSpiral* that leads to depression. The *UpSpiral* does not; it is the opposite of depression. The *DownSpiral* is greatly responsible for our health-related issues because it represents the person in a state of "dis-ease", out of balance, out of synchrony, out of a basic vibration with themselves and the universe.

> People who spend their time in the *DownSpiral* are twice as likely to have a stroke or heart attack.

The basic reason for this is that by playing to your weaknesses in the *DownSpiral*, you disengage from your strengths and get out of alignment with them. Your strengths are your real self. When you are not in alignment with your real self, you are going to experience dysynchrony. This dysynchrony is a vibration of energy that communicates with your body at a cellular level and upsets the balance of the assimilation-elimination activity of the cells. *It inhibits thriving at a cellular level.*

Step One: Awareness

This sounds simple, and it is. When you become aware that there is an *UpSpiral* and a *DownSpiral*, that awareness starts to affect your choices. When you start to "feel worse", you begin to get the idea that you are thinking and feeling something that isn't working. Eventually, you will begin to recognize what thinking and feeling states keep you in an *UpSpiral* and which take you to a *DownSpiral*. The Calendar Exercise, introduced in a few paragraphs, will help with this greatly.

Here are some simple keys. When you are in a *DownSpiral* and you start going "up", you feel relief, sometimes a little, sometimes a lot, but you feel relief. Go toward the relief; move toward what feels better. When you're in an *UpSpiral* and you start going down, you start to feel disconnected, "off", not in touch with yourself. Then, as you continue, you feel worried, anxious, frustrated, aggravated and so on. In an *UpSpiral*, in a good place, you simply feel good.

This is, perhaps, a good place to talk about bliss. There is a lot of

> When you become aware that there is an *UpSpiral* and a *DownSpiral*, that awareness starts to affect your choices.

talk about bliss, getting to your bliss and following your bliss. I'm not really interested in bliss. I want something that is accessible immediately to everyday people. It is the normal, not the super-normal that we're after here. We get too "woo-woo" because we have gotten away from what are just normal states of living. I figure that I'm going to spend eternity in bliss so why not just be human, while I have this wonderful opportunity! If you want bliss, go for it. But what I want is just to "feel good" most all of the time, with maybe a kick or two of bliss once in a while, but not required. Life is so good, just in "feeling good" and I think that's what most people want. We just want to "feel good". There are, I think, too many people wanting to go to some "blissed out" state without mastering just "feeling good". When I ask the average person, "How do you feel?" I don't expect to get, "Oh, I'm blissed". That just isn't normal and I don't believe it's what the human condition is about. I believe that when I ask someone how they feel, I'd like to hear, "I feel good". That's what I want to tell people, "I feel good." The *UpSpiral* is, at its core, about "feeling good", not about exalted states of consciousness. However, the *UpSpiral* is open at the top and you can go there. If you do the work in this book, that's the promise of what you'll get to: "feeling good".

So the reasons for staying in an *UpSpiral* are obvious. The question is really "How do you stay there 95% of the time?" The first thing you have to do is become aware that there is an *UpSpiral* and that you are either there or you're not, most of the time. You can also consider how much and to what degree you are in this *UpSpiral*

Step Two: Decide

As you decide that you want to be in an *UpSpiral* of positivity, you are already setting forces into motion. When it comes to wanting to be in a different state of mind, the "wanting" is very important.

The degree to which you want has to be enough to get you to take notice of whether or not you are in the *UpSpiral*. The first step is awareness the *UpSpiral* exists and knowing whether you are or not in it. The second step *decides* to be there or stay there.

Step Three: The *Emotional Gym*

Exercise positive emotion and start to feel positive emotions. Go back to the material in Chapter 1 and reread the material there on how to work the *Emotional Gym* and to begin to build positive emotion. Do the *Emotional Gym* exercises at the end of each chapter-do them everyday. That is the promise at the beginning of this chapter –they really do work.

Step Four: The Stop Doing Things: The Big Four
You have to make some decisions about what you are not going

> As you decide that you want to be in an *UpSpiral* of positivity, you are already setting forces into motion. When it comes to wanting to be in a different state of mind, the "wanting" is very important.

to do. There are at least four things that I require of my clients. Every time you engage in negative self-talk, stop and do the exercises of the *Emotional Gym.*

1. *Stop all negative self-talk and give up being critical of yourself and others.* Just give it up. Stop it.
2. *Stop blaming others for your problems or any problems.* The negative you see in others is an expression of what is negative, on some level, in you. What you "spot", you "got". The best way to get insight into the blaming game is the work of Byron Katie, cited in her book called **Loving What Is.** This is work that helps you get a hold on how you are projecting what you haven't loved and accepted in yourself. There is no need to discuss this anymore here; Byron Katie's work is superb. If this is a problem for you, that keeps you out of the *UpSpiral*, then get involved in what Byron Katie calls "The Work" and you will never regret that you did.
3. *Give up being the cynic or the critic of the world.*
   Give up being an intellectualized, pessimistic critic of the world. Give up the idea that you need to find out what is wrong about others and the world around you. If you can't give it up forever,

then give it up for awhile. There are people who have made an art form out of finding things that are wrong and shining the light on them. You get what you shine your light on. Be negative and shine your light on the negative, and you get negativity. Pride yourself on "telling it like it is" and you will forever be getting just "what is" as you negatively see it. If you want to be in the *UpSpiral*, then give up being a "critic" of yourself, of others, or the world.

4. ***Turn off the television or be very selective about what you watch, especially the news.*** If you can, turn off the news for a while. You'll be amazed at how much you know about what's going on, that's really important, when you don't watch the news. If you want to be in the *UpSpiral*, for a while, don't spend your time listening to and watching every negative thing that's going on in the world. Just try it for a while. News programs have a lot of space to fill and in doing so, they are also filling your brain with everything that is negative and wrong in the world, so they can fill their news time. If it doesn't give you good feelings, don't watch it, whatever it is, for a while. Step back from filling your mind with negative information and images. They are powerful and they slowly overwhelm the attempt to build a positive mind. Start to be very selective about what you put into your mind. You are probably very selective about your food, about your clothes. Be as selective about the information you "take in", because the brain has to process it and do something with it. Give your brain a break and don't make it absorb and process so much negative information. You are already on overload with negative information. Take a 90 day retreat from negative news and negative information.

The Upward Spiral Calendar.

Get a calendar that you can write on and as you begin each day, from a range of 1-100, put a number on the calendar of where you would like to be in the *UpSpiral*. (Forty-nine and below is actually the *DownSpiral*.) From 50 to 100, write down a number each day where you are shooting for in the Upward Spiral, in terms of the amount of time you want to spend there. Start with where you are and put in a number 3-9 points higher.

The Emotional Scale.

The second number you write down on your calendar is where you want to be on an Emotional Scale. If 1 is despondency and depression, a state in which you attract almost nothing you want to yourself and 100 marks the place of joy and gratitude, where you attract and bring into your life most everything you want, put a subjective number that represents where you want to be on an Emotional Scale.

What are you wanting?

Also, write in the daily box on the calendar, something you are wanting. Just write down a want. As you pay attention to your *UpSpiral* and Emotional Scale and as you increase your score, because you will, watch what happens to what you are "wanting". You are going to find that what you want shows up and happens a lot of the time. And over time, more and more so.

Try it, have a little fun with it.

This exercise begins to create a growing awareness on your part and you begin to set small daily goals and intentions that increase your consciousness about being in the *UpSpiral*.

In the last chapter, Exercise I of the *Emotional Gym* was introduced. The exercise was to feel the feelings of joy, love, happiness, and peace 10 times each, once a day. Remember that you are "pulsing" these emotions for a few seconds each and you are doing this as often as you can throughout your day. They are becoming an ambient background in your life. Dan Gilbert from the Hedonistic Laboratory at Harvard offers that 100 small hits of happiness are more important than large occasional events of happiness over a long period of time. Feeling positive emotions adds to this notion of "100 hits".

The *Emotional Gym* reverses the traditional "cause and effect" nature of positive emotion; you don't need to have a reason to feel a positive emotion contrary to popular belief. Just feel them, hundreds of them, and the cumulative result will be the experience of greater pervasive happiness.

We now build on that first exercise. At my loft in downtown Los Angeles, there is a fire station about two blocks away. The firemen are, at least once a day, out of the firehouse in their big, red, very noisy, very loud "chariots of deliverance" from fire. They not only have sirens but they have added "squawkers", which are extremely loud sirens for making it safely through intersections. And I think they like to use all of the noisemakers, not only for safety, but to let people know that they are riding out to do their jobs. Because, even when the intersections are empty or have little traffic or even little sign of traffic, they use the squawkers at 2, 3 and 4 a.m. when the streets are empty. It is as though they want all of these modern loft dwellers to know that they are on the job, and if they don't get to sleep, neither does anyone else.

I was almost ready to complain to the powers-that-be and then I decided, in the face of what these men and women do, the enormous risks they have to take, and the fact they had to be up at 2 a.m., that I would make the problem of the sirens mine, instead of theirs. Doing so has given me this powerful exercise for the *Emotional Gym-Cued Emotions.*

I decided to be very grateful for these brave, good men and women who would come to save me anytime I called and to feel peace - a great deal of peace - that they were there doing this incredible job that they do. I decided to use the fire engine sirens as a signal, as a "cue" for feeling peace. I reasoned that if I could feel peace in the face of this intruding noise, that I would be able to feel peace anywhere, anytime on call. And that became my goal.

As soon as the siren wound up, I would start to feel a little bit of peace. I would just relax from the immediate tensing up that was going on inside of me and relish feeling that little bit of peace. I would relax the tightening in my jaw and my forehead. I thought about peaceful things. I felt peace in my lower chakra, my groin, and even in my belly. I kept practicing (and, believe me, you get a lot of practice with the sounds of sirens in downtown Los Angeles). I began, over time, to get pretty good at feeling a little bit of peace. Then a little bit peace became a lot more peace as I began to offer a silent prayer for the safety of those firefighters and the victims of fire. The peace grew. Every time the sirens sounded was enough of a noxious stimulus or cue that I would always remember to relax and feel peace. *And then, one day, I forgot.* I didn't notice the sirens. It happened a few more times and I realized that I was feeling an immediate peace, on an unconscious, subliminal level, without even processing it. Whenever the noise seemed like noise or whenever I recognized the cue, I returned to feeling peace.

The fire engine sirens were a "noxious stimuli". It is hardest in the face of noxious stimuli to elicit a positive emotion. That is why negative cues are so good to practice with. However, cues that are noxious aren't the only the cues you use to practice a positive emotion. The cues can be pleasant as well. The important thing is whether or not the cue will act as a reminder for you to practice feeling the positive emotion. The cue needs to be distinct and particular enough that you can begin to use it as a signal that will remind you to practice the positive emotions.

Some cues might be:

A telephone ring = peace

A pet = joy

Sitting down to a meal = gratitude

A stop sign = love

Find the cues that will remind you, throughout the day, to practice a positive emotion. Then after a while, change the cue, because you will likely get used to it. Using a noxious cue, or an unpleasant one, makes the practice of the positive emotion a little more difficult, but it locks the feelings in more quickly.

The important thing to remember when you practice positive emotions is that you need to do it frequently, daily and consistently. Each time you practice feeling positive emotions, you remind yourself to do it and it generalizes or spreads to a wider and wider field in your life.

The positive feelings you are practicing are building a buffer against negative feelings. Negative feelings are less likely to "stick" and if they do stick, they become less toxic much more quickly. In short, you will feel less badly, more often. Practice positive emotions and you will spend more time in positive emotions.

The Outcomes of the *UpSpiral*.

You are more creative.

You solve problems faster and better.

You learn more quickly.

You score higher on every test of well-being.

You score higher on every test of life-satisfaction.

You thrive at a cellular level.

You play to your strengths rather than your weaknesses.

You are two times less likely to experience a heart attack or stroke, as contrasted with those who spend most of their time in a *DownSpiral*.

As you finish reading this chapter, you are confronted with a choice. How do you want to live? In an *UpSpiral* or a *DownSpiral*? If you are still unsure that you can live in an *UpSpiral*, try it for 90 days.

Until recently, we have not known that living in an *UpSpiral* all of the time was possible. We are on the verge of a new consciousness, a new way of seeing and knowing our own lives. Life in the *DownSpiral* of fear and "victimhood" has not netted us what it seemed to have promised. Being intellectually cynical and critical of life has not proven to be healthy or productive. Many of the myths of our parents are not true, especially those which concern suffering and the proverbial "no pain, no gain" mantras. It is just as true that good things have come easier for many people and not by accident or by birth-right. Happy people in an *UpSpiral* have always been around, getting what they wanted out of life, but we just have not studied them closely enough, with enough scientific rigor and precise research. We know much, much more about depression and pathology.

There can be an overriding, powerful, lasting *UpSpiral* in your life that defines the best of who you are and gets it out of you. It is not a matter of finding the way. That is explained here. It is a matter of choice. Yours!

Workout #2: The *Emotional Gym* for the *UpSpiral*

1. Continue to do the exercise you learned in the previous chapter. Feel the five emotions of gratitude, love, peace, joy, and hope. Do the pulsing exercise throughout the day. Make these emotions the ambient sound track of your daily life. Just make that a regular work out for 90 days and throughout each day. Remember to "pulse" the emotions over and over and over again until these emotions become the ambient soundtrack of your life.

2. We begin to build a greater degree of familiarity with these emotions and with building them into an *UpSpiral*, by selecting some cues that will act to remind you to go to a certain feeling. A cue is something that will remind you to feel one of the five feel-

ings. Each feeling needs its own cue. Every time the cue presents itself, feel the feeling to which it is attached.

To review, the cue might be the ring of a telephone and the feeling may be joy, if that works for you.

A physician working with me had to put on surgical clothes several times a day, so every time he changed his clothes he felt the feeling of love.

A red light could be a cue for peace.

Noxious cues are harder to use. This was the example I gave earlier of hearing the fire siren outside my window and using as a cue to feel "peace". This is harder to do but it can transform something that seems negative into something that is far more bearable. A horn, a siren, traffic, whatever works can be a "noxious" or unpleasant cue that tells you to go to one of your five lead feelings.

Feel the feeling of gratitude, love, peace, joy, or hope. Again, you are still working on immediacy. The idea is to go to the feeling immediately. See how fast you can feel the feeling you are working with. It does not matter if you don't feel a great deal of the feeling at this point. What matters is that you feel the feeling, on a scale of 1 -10, at a 3 or 4. If 10 is feeling the feeling of gratitude very intensely, just feel it at a 2, 3 or 4 and then hold the feeling, go back to it, and feel it for an even longer period of time.

As you begin to hold the feeling and to go back to it, you are starting to exercise the second dimension of a feeling - duration. Duration is making the feeling last longer, but not necessarily at a more intense level.

UpSpiral Summary

To grow a positive mind from which you become who you really are and from which you attract into your life what you really want, you have to learn how to stay in an *UpSpiral*. Nothing anyone wants can be found in a *DownSpiral*.

The *UpSpiral* is a spiral of positive emotion and energy and you can be in that spiral 100% of the time. The *UpSpiral* is a spiral that is a positive frame of mind, a state of mind that sees things from a positive perspective. It has been described as optimism, but it is more than that; it is an energy that is also a flow that builds psychological capital.

Pessimism is an overwhelming factor in health-related issues and in personal success and achievement. It really is our number one health problem and the greatest deterrent of well-being and life satisfaction.

Neuroplasticity is the ability of the brain to grow new pathways, not only for physical movement or memory functions, but new ways of knowing and being that constitute a higher degree of human consciousness. It is the ability of your brain to rewire and reprogram itself. The growing and building of positive emotion creates an *UpSpiral*.

The brain ages, but, like fine wine, it does not have to decline. The brain develops throughout all of life. There does not have to be decline. Rather, the brain, as a developmental task in the second half of life, transfers the psychic energy of things like short-term memory into things like "getting the larger picture" so that life will be lived on a plane of wider and fuller satisfaction.

You don't have to be pessimistic to think critically. You have to use your strengths and play to your strengths in the *UpSpiral* and you will think more critically, more creatively, and you will be far more likely to take critical and decisive action without fear of retribution. These strengths will be talked about in the next chapter, *StrengthSmart*.

Our lives, as they are, give us enough contrast to know what we want, without having to experience a greater misery to know that we want to feel good. *We believe too much in the essential nature of opposites. The delicate shades and experiences of our lives are enough to move us to what we want, if we believe they are. All of the drama just isn't essential unless we believe that it is.*

People who spend their time in the downward spiral are twice as likely to have a stroke or heart attack.

When you become aware that there is an *UpSpiral* and a *DownSpiral*, that awareness starts to affect your choices.

As you decide that you want to be in an *UpSpiral* of positivity, you are already setting forces into motion. When it comes to wanting to be in a different state of mind, the "wanting" is very important.

StrengthSmart

By knowing and using your strengths everyday, you can raise your happiness set-point, your emotional set-up, and become happier and more content.

Our weaknesses change very little over a lifetime. Our strengths, which when identified and validated, are infinitely malleable.

This is the quote I have on my business cards. I'd take the quote a step further. Our weaknesses change, at the most, over the course of a life time no more than 3-7% and the upper ranges of that figure are only for those who consistently go to some kind of 12 step group or self-growth experience over a considerable length of time.

Weaknesses or defects of character - call them what you will - don't change very much because they are really not supposed to change; they are important indicators of the other end of the stick. The stick which is a character trait has two ends; one is the weakness and the other is the strength. A weakness is the opposite of a strength.

Every strength has a weakness. If you do away with the weakness, you do away with a signpost or cue to the strength. The weakness simply points to the strength.

Our weaknesses change, at the most, over the course of a life time no more than 3-7% and the upper ranges of that figure are only for those who consistently go to some kind of 12 step group or self-growth experience over a considerable length of time.

A strength also has an exaggeration and it has an absence; it has four dimensions. But for our purposes here we will see a strength as the other end of the stick from a weakness.

One quick way to get an idea of your strengths is to list your weaknesses. We all tend to be better at listing our weaknesses than we are at knowing our strengths. If you do this, what will emerge will be a vague idea of your strengths. What's more, these strengths are much more accessible to you than you might believe. The neuro-pathways that are strengths began forming when you were two years old, at a time when you lost the largest number of brain cells you will ever lose. The brain formed based on the genetic code of the individual and in relationship to the influences of the environment. The pathways of our strengths are solidly sewn into the warp and woof of our personality. They are the basic designs and weave of the fabric of who we are.

Know your strengths and you get a pretty good idea of what your real self is. Your real self is your strengths in work, play and growth. Your strengths emerge when you are in an *UpSpiral* and your weaknesses play when you are in a *DownSpiral*.

When you know and use your strengths you feel happy and you feel good. But most people have only a faint idea of their strengths. Because strengths feel so natural and often so easy for us, we tend to be dismissive of them. We want to work "harder" to prove that we are deserving and instead make life much more difficult than it needs to be and playing to our weaknesses makes us work much,

much harder. Our strengths make most things much easier. And our strengths work together to keep us in an *UpSpiral*, once we get into the habit of using them.

Your strengths emerge when you are in an *UpSpiral* and your weaknesses play when you are in a *DownSpiral*. *When you know and use your strengths you feel happy and you feel good.*

However, when we are stressed, in the face of difficulties and challenges, we play to our weaknesses rather than our strengths, because we have the idea that we can fight or flee better with our weaknesses. Our strengths engage us in a challenge and are far more likely to inspire our success, or if the challenge isn't particularly good for us, they help disengage us from the challenge.

We have spent a lot of time shining the light on weaknesses and what is wrong, believing that the way to make progress is to fix weaknesses and character defects. In fact, shining the light on them grows them. If you want to grow your weaknesses, just pay a little more attention and they will oblige you. It is only when we try alternatives to our weaknesses that they begin to diminish simply out of lack of use and attention. Focus on your weaknesses and you fan them into a flame.

Dr. Jeffrey Schwartz, in work with Obsessive-Compulsive Disorder (OCD) patients, showed how the neuroplasticity of the brain develops in accord with what we focus on and give our attention to. Dr. Schwartz explains how in quantum physics this is called the Xeno Effect. It means that attention of focus slows down the processing of thoughts and the building of the neural circuitry that supports them. Your strengths already exist as focused neural super highways because they are the way you have developed. But you may not have known how to use these pathways, to access them, or how to grow them because you didn't know they existed.

We are a culture driven to believe that we have to work on our weaknesses and become a balanced, well-rounded person. At the cost of giving the attention to what is good in us and growing our real potential, we spend countless hours and lots of dollars on trying to fix what is wrong. If we can't fix it in ourselves, we believe that we can fix our partners or our kids. Usually what we're busy fixing in somebody else is what we wish we could fix in ourselves. It just doesn't work.

The parents I speak to and work with are, at first, disturbed to find out what little influence they have over their adolescent children, especially when it comes to changing their weaknesses or problems. They really have no direct influence over changing weaknesses. They simply can't and usually these "fixer" parents only make the problems worse by shining the light on them. Teachers either start the problem or continue it by focusing undue attention on what's wrong with a child, and what they think has to be fixed or changed. The only way a teacher or parents can change a child is by acknowledging and building on a child's strengths through encouragement and positive expectation. Instead of concentrating on their weaknesses, teachers and parents should be giving the child hope and encouragement to grow in a direction that is the expression of the child's strengths. What is true for you is also true for the child.

However, if you haven't had the experience of growing your own strengths and learning to play to them in the face of challenge or adversity, it is highly unlikely that you will be able to do that for a child. You can't model what you don't know. It's important to stress that children learn from example. They are going to find the strength or weakness they have that matches yours and follow that example. If they don't see what is positive, they will model the negative strength. We both know how good your children are in modeling what's wrong with you. That becomes all the more reason to struggle to force it out of them, in some vain attempt to rid yourself of your own weaknesses.

This can all be much easier. Focus on the strengths, grow the strengths and the strengths will manage the weaknesses and after a time weaknesses will diminish and become more manageable. Those mental circuits in the brain decrease only by non-use, not by a head-on assault. However, we never want them to disappear. *We never want weaknesses to be erased.* They are too important as signposts to our strengths; they are the shadows of our strengths.

Weaknesses are the end of the character stick that warns us when we are off track. When we go in a direction for very long that is not in alignment with our real self, our weaknesses are called to attention to warn us that we are off track. First, we get negative feelings; we just don't feel good or we don't feel right. Then we see our weakness start to emerge. If that doesn't warn us, if the weaknesses can't get the message to us, then we start getting sick in a myriad of ways. I wish this was more complex. If it were it might be more believable, but it's just not that complex. It's frighteningly simple. Play to your weaknesses and you get sick because you are out of alignment with your real self. In this state of non-alignment, you will find yourself in a *DownSpiral* and you will get sick.

Play to your strengths, stay in an *UpSpiral*. Grow your strengths and you will feel good and you will be healthier. Get it? Do you want to get it? If you want to get it, you will and you will grow in the direction I am suggesting. If you don't want to get it, you won't, until you are ready. You can get it from a standpoint of happiness and joy or you can get it from being miserable. It's your choice, but you don't have to be miserable to "get it".

Ten Strengths
In our work here, you will be directed to two tests that will help

you find out what your strengths are and how you approach using them. Think about this for a minute. Instead of giving you a test to find out what's wrong with you, these are tests to find out what's right and what's good about you. These are tests to tell you what you're good at and capable of getting better at. They are validating and hope-giving tests that point you in the direction of your real self. Knowing even just 10 of your strengths will give you a much better idea of who you really are. Work those 10 strengths, play to them every day and you will discover even more and more about your real self. You will be in an *UpSpiral* and this spiral is open at the top.

The **Strengthsfinder** test was developed by Dr. Donald Clifton several years ago and is the primary measure used by the Gallup Research Institute in their work with both business and education. The **Strengthsfinder** test (version 2.0) identifies strengths that are more specifically action-oriented. These are strengths that identify something that you are good at and describe a general category of ability that can be grown and developed and that can be applied with great specificity.

At the end of the chapter, you will be given an assignment to take this test and the directions about where to find it. It will be an invaluable resource for our work here.

The second test is called the **VIA Signature Strengths Inventory** which was developed by Dr. Martin Seligman and Dr. Chris Peterson. They are the authors of the first nosology of strengths called **<u>Character Strengths and Virtues (CSV).</u>** It is for positive psychology and health what the **DSM IV** (the Diagnostic and Statistical Manual) is for diagnosing pathology. It is an initial attempt to put into categories, with descriptions, a manual for classifying strengths. While it will undoubtedly be changed and updated over the years, it is a valuable tool even now. What is important to realize is, that like pathology, strengths are related. The **CSV** manual is the first attempt to identify and categorize strengths and all of their variations and it will tighten up in later versions. It is an *extremely valuable* resource.

The **Values In Action (VIA)** is a values-oriented strengths test. It identifies five signature strengths and describes strengths that are also core values as well as ways of perceiving and behaving that you are best at.

Both tests have been widely used and are highly reliable. The combination of these two tests identifies 10 strength areas that can be used in combination. You will find that you have strengths to deal with any area of your life and any challenge that you might confront. Your strengths are a unique expression of you and the way you go about living your life, being you. At the end of this chapter you will be directed to a website where you can take this test.

The more you develop these strengths and get used to using what is actually yours, the more time you will spend in the *UpSpiral* because using your strengths helps you stay there. The longer you are in an *UpSpiral*, the more used to being there you get. And the more used to being there you are, the more sensitive you become to anything that moves you away from the *UpSpiral*. In a way, you start to feel like you are in a particular vibrational state and you become sensitive to anything that lowers your vibration.

Basic to being *StrengthSmart* is the realization that strengths hold a significant key to staying in the *UpSpiral*. This is the promise: your strengths, actively engaged, always keep you in an *UpSpiral*. They also provide all of the analytical and critical skills you need without having to go into a *DownSpiral* of pessimism to be able to think critically and/or to be sufficiently scrutinizing of decision-making in your life.

The more you develop these strengths and get used to using what is actually yours, the more time you will spend in the *UpSpiral* because using your strengths helps you stay there.

This is the promise: your strengths, actively engaged, will always keep you in an *UpSpiral*. They also provide all of the analytical and critical skills you need without having to go into a *DownSpiral* of pessimism to be able to think critically and/or to be sufficiently scrutinizing of decision-making in your life.

Strengths As Lenses

I suggest to my clients that they use their strengths as lenses, sort of like putting on "rose colored glasses", only these strengths are real. Look through the lens of a particular strength, think from and talk from that lens. What does the strength say about this or that issue? Each lens - or strength - creates a usually small, but highly significant shift in attention and focus. You start to see the challenge differently. By the time you have gone through all 10 strengths, you will have a new perspective with which to view any problem or challenge. Things will look differently and you will very likely start to change your approach.

The Basic Alignment of Strengths

One of the most significant contributions of **Character Strengths and Virtues** is that it is a value-based strengths test. This means that the strengths tested there are also basic core values to the person. The "strengths as values" provide a guide to what one must be aligned with in the self. While the **VIA** test gives a read out of what is called one's top five Signature Strengths the significance of the top 10 are very close. But working with 10 strengths all at once becomes unwieldy. Whether you look at your top five or your top 10 strengths, you are looking at an initial measure that is telling you something about your Real Self. I treat the ego-self as the adaptive self; we grew up with it and learned to adapt to the world as best we could, using both strengths and weaknesses. Usually, we were pulled a lot in the direction of weaknesses, especially in times of stress and difficulty.

The greater your alignment, your consistency and your focus is on your strengths, the more in alignment with your Real Self you are going to feel. You will feel more in sync, more in control, more in harmony, more like you are "in your own skin". It is when we play to our weaknesses that we begin to feel "out of sync", disconnected, out of alignment, anxious, frustrated, and in a state of discord.

Playing to your strengths keeps you in an *UpSpiral* while playing to your weaknesses puts you into a *DownSpiral*. Ignoring your strengths causes you to flatline; there just seems to be no "umph" in life. You experience being rudderless with no anchor.

Alignment with your strengths is a key part of being and remaining in the *UpSpiral*. For every client with whom I work who comes to me with something like, "I don't know who I am, I don't know my self, I don't know what I want, I don't know who is the real me", the identification of and validation of strengths is a key answer to these questions. Know and relish your strengths as values and you, in a very basic way, know "who" you are. You stop asking questions like, "Who am I?" You know. Your strengths give you that information. You don't know everything, but you have a compass to guide you and an internal sense of direction.

Can these strengths change? Yes, they do change to some minor degree. However, the change is not so important. Anytime you are pulling on one strength and using and growing that strength, you are pulling on all of the others. They are all connected. Grow one and you grow them all, to some degree.

Your strengths are you. They are the emerging points of the real

> *The greater your alignment, your consistency and your focus is on your strengths, the more in alignment with your Real Self you are going to feel. You will feel more in sync, more in control, more in harmony, more like you are "in your own skin". It is when we play to our weaknesses that we begin to feel "out of sync", disconnected, out of alignment, anxious, frustrated, and in a state of discord.*

you. Perhaps the **VIA** and the **Strengthsfinder** tests will not absolutely give a total, complete "right on" answer, but they will get you very, very close assessments. The rest you can find out for yourself as you work with your identified strengths.

Knowing and validating one's strengths is enormously important. Many people scour their beings, trying to find out why they are the way they are, in an effort to explain weaknesses and problems. Far more effective is to scour one's strengths, to put the attention and the focus there, to shine the light on one's strengths. These strengths are infinitely malleable. They grow and grow and they are the source of genius in each individual person. *Always, the problems we encounter do not lie in our weaknesses but occur instead in the absent use of our available strengths.*

Play to your strengths for 20 years and you will learn a lot about how they can help you, who you really are, and how to best grow them and make them your focus. Do this and you will become your own genius.

In the Soviet Union, an experiment was done using hypnosis to enlarge upon people's artistic skills. Three groups of people were chosen to participate on the basis of having some proven artistic ability. They were hypnotized to believe that they were great artists and then painted a series of four paintings. The results were remarkable. The growth in ability from one painting to the next was significantly marked. Many of the works were artistically sophisticated enough to be exhibited in galleries and sold.

For us, the importance of the experiment shows the power of shining the light on a strength, of making an ability a focus and growing that ability. Granted these abilities were more in the area of what we understand as talent, rather than values, but the important insight here is the value of focus and believing. Finding out that you have a strength is enormously validating. Validate the strength and shine the light on the strength and it starts to grow. As strengths start to grow, weaknesses begin to be left behind. While they may never completely disappear, they become much more manageable.

Find Out What Your Strengths Are: Take the Tests

1. The **VIA Signature Strengths** Test can be found at www.Authentic Happiness.org. Take the test.

2. The **Strengthsfinder** test can be found in the book **Strengthsfinder 2.0** by Tom Rath published by Gallup Press. Buy the book and take the **Strengthsfinder** test there. You will be given a lengthy and elegant description of the test and the strengths and a code that will give you access to the online computerized test. Just follow the directions. This is an invaluable asset for you.

How do we grow strengths?

First, and most important, find out what yours are and then choose to use them in every day life. In his book, **Authentic Happiness**, Dr. Martin Seligman discusses how the engagement of strengths relates directly to happiness. Think from them, reason from them, and build them into your life. Here are a few of myriad ways I have learned to help people do that.

Focus on one strength.

For one month, take one strength and focus on that strength. Write it on a piece of paper, put in on the refrigerator or in the bathroom or anywhere where you will be sure to see it often. Carry it in your wallet or purse. Make the strength conspicuous.

My Daily Plan

My idea for this exercise is credited to Dr. Joe Dispenza from the movie, *What The Bleep*. Get a journal and write a plan every day, of just a few sentences, of how you want your day to go and how you want to use a particular strength. Call it **My Daily Plan**. The book, **Plans to the Universe and the Answers Back**, which was designed to accompany this book, is a daily guide to that practice. Get the book and follow it along one day at time.

This "daily plan" has proven to be enormously beneficial. What strength or strengths do you want to use or grow? You will be surprised at how your day will "pull" on those very strengths. Some days you'll forget about what you wrote, and then in the evening, when you do another exercise that will be explained here, called **The Gratitude Scan**, you'll realize how what you asked for actually happened. **The Gratitude Scan** is an exercise for the *Emotional Gym* which asks that you practice ending your day with the positive emotion of gratitude. When you go to sleep, the unconscious mind or subjective mind picks up where the conscious mind leaves off, but not on a content or thought level. It picks up on the emotional level you leave your day with as you go to sleep. It is your feeling state that sets up the first part of your sleep architecture and has a lasting effect on your sleep throughout the night. It is in **The Gratitude Scan** that you will see how your day has gone remarkably like what you set up in your **Daily Plan**.

Most often, over time, and not such a long time, you're going to find that what you ask for is what you get. Intentionality is every-thing. You create what you think, but you don't create from your superficial thinking unless that superficial thinking represents a deeper consciousness or intentionality. Honestly, what is "off the top of your head" is not necessarily superficial. It is best to keep this exercise somewhat "light". How would you like your day to go and how would you like to be in that day, using your strengths? If you do this exercise every day, you are in for some surprises. As soon as you decide that you create your world, you will.

The Scrapbook

Scrapbooking has become enormously popular and it is very sig-nificant. *A scrapbook is about identity.* It preserves the bits and pieces of our lives and reflects back to us what we have done and are doing, where we have been and are currently, in our lives. A scrapbook has a strong voice. It will talk to you. It is an invaluable resource for a sense of identity. And so it is with strengths. Get a scrapbook and divide it into 10 sections, five for your **VIA** strengths and five for your **Strengthsfinder** strengths. You can write in the scrapbook and use it as a journal and save articles, pictures, and anything else that reminds you of a strength. Cut out words and save the tickets to a movie that reminded you of something about a strength. Build an identity around a strength. This is a great exercise for anyone, but it can be used especially well in a group setting or in a school setting to teach and develop an identity around strengths. Be sure to cut out or draw pictures of what you want. Give what you want most – that is, what is most important to you, a page of its own. Don't be afraid to "want". And keep your nose out of the "how". The "how" is not your business, at least not at first. The "how" will unfold. Many folks have done this exercise, forgotten completely about what they cut out or pasted on a page or a picture they stored in a "want" box, only to find out years later, upon opening it, after it was long forgotten, that they had gotten almost everything that was in the box in one way or another.

Scrapbooking could take an entire chapter, even an entire book in terms of its significance, but there just isn't room here. To sum it all up, it is a significantly important strategy.

Get a Strengths Partner

Find someone else who is interested in growing their strengths. Have a five minute conversation five days a week with the person about how you are growing a particular strength. Talk about how you are using it. You can talk briefly once a day during the week days or you can meet once during the week and talk for a longer length of time. Keep your conversation strengths-centered around a single simple question, "How are you using your strengths?" Keep the focus on strengths and solutions rather than on the problems.

Vibration and Strengths

We are going to spend a good deal more time talking about "vibration" in the chapter on your *VibeCore*, but let's begin an initial discussion here by looking at strengths as a vibration. If you can entertain even the slightest notion that your own personal energy is some kind of "vibration", then you will recognize when you are playing to your strengths, that you are more finely tuned to the vibration that is your real self. Esther Hicks introduced me to this idea of "vibration" and to the notion that we are, all of us, essentially a vibration. We talk about our "vibes" or the "vibes" we get from others, so we already have a sensitivity to this reality of vibrations. Your highest and best vibrations are the use of your strengths; you vibrate most with who you are and who you attract, by the nature of the vibration, people and situations which match the vibration of your strengths. This is part of what helps to pull you higher and higher in your own *UpSpiral*. Think of yourself as essentially pure energy, and that you vibrate at a certain, perfect speed or velocity when you are at your best using your strengths. This would certainly be when you are using your strengths and are also plugged into others who are using theirs and validating yours.

A vibration is harmonious; our vibration signals a harmoniously aligned place in our own beings. Remember the research done by Fredrickson and the finding that we thrive at a cellular level when we are in the *UpSpiral*. Another way of saying this might be that our vibration is such that we are not fighting our own well-being but are in harmony with the basic activity of our bodies at a cellular level. In the place of a higher, more harmonious vibration, there is less stress and the body can perform its functions at a much higher level of efficacy. Our cells are happier!

Let's further consider that we really do draw people to us who are on a kind of similar "wavelength". We attract them through the use of our strengths. We are going to attract and get along with people who are most "in sync" with us. Most of our energy or vibrational level, perhaps with different strengths, will be able to be exercised complementarily.

When we play to the opposite side of strengths, to our weaknesses, we end up attracting people of discord, people who are divisive, and who, in a sense, "bring us down", or repel the people that we would want to attract. What is this, except lowering the nature of our energy? Playing to weaknesses draws to you people who are not a match on one level or another. Believe me. They aren't good for you, they don't offer you what you need, they hold you down, keep you back, and catch you up in things that you have no business being a part of. When we say, "he pulls me down", "she is a drag", "he sucks my energy", we are, without always knowing it, sensitive on a vibrational level to people who are not pulling from their strengths and not encouraging our own. To the contrary, they draw the worst out of us, while we wonder what it is that is "pulling us down" so much. It is not difficult to think of times when other people's negative energy or vibration affected us negatively in ways that were not healthy for us to remain in their presence or their association.

The more time you spend in an *UpSpiral*, the more time you play to your strengths. These strengths used individually and collectively create a buffer zone against negativity. It will take longer for a negative situation to "get to you", you will be resistant to the stress it can create at a physical level, and you will have a greater "reaction time/space buffer" to something that is negative. You won't react as quickly, you won't jump at it emotionally so fast, and it won't negatively affect you so quickly. It will not affect you for as long or at the emotional depth which it used to. The buffer that is developed by being in the *UpSpiral* both resists and heals negative emotion and negative experiencing. Increase your vibration by playing to your strengths and you will increase your resistance to what is negative and to what brings you down. When you do get down, you will spend much less time there.

In fact - and this is really the amazing part - your strengths are a perfectly designed, unique package that you will find you have to deal with *any* challenge. *Put them all together or use them one a time or in pairs or multiple combinations and your strengths will handle any and all challenges in your life.* Draw on your strengths and play to them.

In fact - and this is really the amazing part - your strengths are a perfectly designed, unique package that you will find you have to deal with *any* challenge. *Put them all together or use them one at a time or in pairs or multiple combinations and your strengths will handle any and all challenges in your life.* Draw on your strengths and play to them.

Research and Study Your Strengths.

If you go on the internet, you will find, probably to your amazement, a vast amount of resources that exist for any single one of your strengths. It may even seem overwhelming. In many cases there will be whole groups dedicated to uses for this strength, or places that have researched or people who are eager to write about them. The resources around your strengths are inexhaustible. Lots and lots of people in the world are thinking about strengths.

The reason that there is so much information about our strengths is that your strengths are connected to larger values and it is these values that are essential to world peace and world order.

A parting word about strengths. You really have to know what your strengths are and how to play to them to discover a sense of your authentic self, who you really are. They are guides to an enormous world of self-discovery. Enjoy your strengths because when you claim them and play to them you will become happier and you will be building psychological capital that will help you get what you want in the world. What is most important is that they will help you align with the magnificently created self you really are and the vibration, harmony, energy, and vitality that increasingly lead you to greater discoveries.

Workout #3: The *Emotional Gym* for *StrengthSmart*

First review the *Emotional Gym* Workout Exercises in the last two chapters. Continue to use the "pulsing exercise" and the cues for emotions. These take a while to condition in, so keep doing them regularly

This exercise involves both thinking and feeling. Whenever you feel down, low, not at ease, or just not in tune or in sync with your-self, focus on your thinking and see *how* you are thinking. See how you might need to change your thinking if you are thinking nega-tively. Byron Katie's book, **Loving What Is**, is an excellent resource to help you get a hold on how you are actually thinking, if recognizing your negative thinking is a problem for you.

Even if you can't immediately change a negative thought, you can make a choice to move to a better feeling place. Let a negative thought be a cue to feel a positive feeling, but not an overdone one. Again, start small and just go from a negative thought to a little bit of a positive emotion. Use the positive emotion that is easiest for you to get to, the one that seems to come most naturally. Go to that feeling, feel a little of that feeling several times and then make it last for a while.

Go to a Strength

There are three kinds of negative thinking that you can begin to target.

1. *Thinking critically about yourself or others*
2. *Blaming others or circumstances for your own circumstances*
3. *Being an elite "intellectual critic" – the judge of the world.*

When you find any of these kinds of thinking occurring, go to a positive emotion, feel the positive emotion, and then identify the strength. From there, you can begin to think and reason: what do your strengths tell you? How are they talking to you?

StrengthsSmart Exercises
Use Strengths as a lens.

In considering a challenge or an issue for which you want a solu-tion, treat each of your strengths as a lens on a pair of glasses and look at the issue through the eyes of the strength. You are actually "thinking" from a different part of your brain and if we could get a MRI scan of your brain, you would actually see your brain thinking from a different place. See the challenge from the perspective of a strength.

Have a Conversation with a Strength

As crazy as this sounds, have an imaginary conversation with one or a set of your strengths. Ask them a question. Then have an imaginary conversation with each one of these and listen. Wait and see what answer comes to your mind.

Strengths As Heroes

In a like manner, find three or four heroes that you believe have your strengths. It is helpful to even find a picture of each of your heroes. Then have an imaginary conversation with each of these and listen to what they have to tell you. The conversation will surprise you, even if it is occurring in your own imagination. Of course, if you believe in a collective unconscious and that we are all joined together in some way, the answers you get may not be entirely of your own making. At any rate, it is a fun and revealing exercise to use, to get more fully tapped into using your strengths.

StrengthSmart Summary

Our weaknesses change, at the most, over the course of a life time no more than 3-7% and the upper ranges of that figure are only for those who consistently go to some kind of 12 step group or self-growth experience over a considerable length of time.

Your strengths emerge when you are in an *UpSpiral* and your weaknesses play when you are in a *DownSpiral*.
When you know and use your strengths you feel happy and you feel good.

The more you develop these strengths and get used to using what is actually yours, the more time you will spend in the *UpSpiral* because using your strengths helps you stay there.

This is the promise: your strengths, actively engaged, always keep you in an *UpSpiral*. They also provide all of the analytical and critical skills you need without having to go into a *DownSpiral* of pessimism to be able to think critically and/or to be sufficiently scrutinizing of decision-making in your life.

The greater your alignment, your consistency and your focus is on your strengths, the more in alignment with your Real Self you are going to feel. You will feel more in sync, more in control, more in harmony, more like you are "in your own skin". It is when we play to our weaknesses that we begin to feel "out of sync", disconnected, out of alignment, anxious, frustrated, and in a state of discord.

In fact - and this is really the amazing part - your strengths are a perfectly designed, unique package that you will find you have to deal with *any* challenge. *Put them all together or use them one a time or in pairs or multiple combinations and your strengths will handle any and all challenges in your life.* Draw on your strengths and play to them.

VibeCore

**Your *VibeCore* is at the heart of you and can grow.
As it increases, you get more of what you want.
Your *VibeCore* is the most significant predictor
of what you will get in your life.**

Before you read further, do this exercise: give yourself your first subjective *VibeCore Score*. Add your *VibeCore Score* to your daily calendar exercise and with your *UpSpiral* and Emotional Scale numbers.

1. On a scale from 1 to 100, if 1 is having no clue what you want and 100 is knowing precisely what you want, give yourself a subjective score of where you are.

2. On a scale from 1 to 100, if 1 is having no hope that you will ever get what you want in life and 100 is being absolutely certain, "you know that you know that you know", give yourself a subjective score of where you are.

3. On a scale from 1 to 100, if 1 is being very isolated and holding on and hoarding whatever you have and 100 is letting go, being open, and sharing who and what you are easily and freely, give yourself a subjective score of where you are. A 1 is being totally uptight and a 100 is just letting go and letting it happen. Where are you?

Now, without getting absolutely black and white mathematical, give yourself a kind of subjective, mental score of the combination of all three of these. This is your *VibeCore Score*.

Where would you rank yourself? How closely is the match between knowing what you want and believing that you will get it? Your *VibeCore Score* is the single most important factor in your subjective judgment for predicting your happiness and it's also a clear guide to how you are feeling on an unconscious level. Your *VibeCore* is the place where you are essentially coming from. It is your "vibe". The higher your *VibeScore*, the stronger and fuller is your positive mind. It relates to whether you draw people to you, leave them where they are, or repel them away from you. Your 'vibe' plugs you into certain situations and it leads you away from others. Your *VibeCore* is kind of like your inner magnet. It defines what you will bring into your life, what you will allow in. It also defines the "vibe" you are putting out. It is like an electro magnet. The greater the electrical energy that flows through the magnet, the stronger its pull. Your *VibeCore* is about the pull of your vibe based upon the energy or vibration it expresses. Think about it. You have undoubtedly been sensitive for a long time to the "vibes" another person puts out. When we tune in and become aware, they are just

The higher your *VibeScore*, the stronger and fuller is your positive mind". It relates to whether you draw people to you, leave them where they are, or repel them away from you. Your 'vibe' plugs you into certain situations and it leads you away from others. Your *VibeCore* is kind of like your inner magnet. It defines what you will bring into your life, what you will allow in. It also defines the "vibe" you are putting out. It is like an electro magnet. The greater the electrical energy that flows through the magnet, the stronger its pull.

there. You have a vibe as well and it comes from your *VibeCore*. That *VibeCore* is the match between knowing what you want and believing that you will get it. It sounds simple, and it really is. Know what you want and believe that you will get it. Once more, as your *VibeScore* starts to increase (and it will increase over time) you will bring into your life more of what you want.

There are three essential questions:

1. How do I really know what I want and how do I know what I think I want is *really* what I want? How do I get precise about it?

2. How do I come to believe that I'm going to get it? I mean, *really* believe it?

3. How do I stay open to the variety of ways this can come into my life and to the variety of ways I can create it and that it can come to me?

$VibeCore$ Score = Wanting x Believing x Openness (letting go)

Here are the answers!

1. How do I really know what I want and how do I know what I think I want is really what I want? How do I get precise about it? **To know what you want consistently over a period of time, in such a way that you really own it, you have to stay in the UpSpiral.** The *DownSpiral* will point you in the direction of what you want. It will give you powerful desires, but it will not sustain your consciousness of those desires. You will lose sight of them in the *DownSpiral* and you will have no real hope that they are even possible. And that's if you can even begin to believe that your desires are possible at all.

For example, an addict often hits a *DownSpiral* bottom before really knowing that what he wants is not there and then has to take sometimes drastic steps to get out the *DownSpiral* to avoid "using" again. Addicts usually have to hit a *DownSpiral* bottom; not everyone else does in order to know what they want. Get out of the

DownSpiral as soon as you know what you want and move toward the *UpSpiral.* Your may need to go back to the chapters on the *Emotional Gym* and the *UpSpiral* - and spend some time there - learning that material.

You come to know- really know- what you want and desire by being in the *UpSpiral* and by becoming *StrengthSmart-* using your strengths reflexively. Addicts use the opposite of their strengths, their character defects, to sustain their addiction. Strengths and defects are opposite ends of the same stick.

You really come to know what you deeply want and desire from spending some time and practice being in an UpSpiral of emotion and playing to your strengths. Here is a strong caveat to coaches, therapists, trainers and teachers: Don't assume your clients know what they want. There is no sense in finding a new job or a new relationship if you take the same discontent with self and the same unrealistic baggage to the next destination. Sometimes you just have to do that to learn, but most of the time, it's really not necessary and an enormous waste of time and resources.

If you have validated your strengths, if you know them and have come to use them reflexively, you already realize that wants and desires have started to bubble-up to the top. They just do, when you come from an *UpSpiral* and play off your strengths. In fact, playing off your strengths in a positive way lets you know what you really want and illuminates your deepest desires and longings. Play to your strengths, find your desires, and you will be rewarded with a gold mine of rich, life enhancing desires that increase an eagerness to live and an aliveness to life.

People have come to me with no clue about what they wanted. Others have told me that they didn't want anything, that they were satisfied, and that they had everything they wanted. That's a shame, I tell them, because they're either flat lining or dead without the good sense to lie down. There is nothing positive about having no desires or wants. Even monks and mystics who preach "no desire", "no attachments" have the desire for peace, oneness, or union with God. They also have desires for love and caring and human community as well as a host of other desires. The issue is being wrongly attached to desire, not the desire in and of itself. You were created to want and to desire. You will spend eternity in union with God. Enjoy the experience of human desire and wanting while you're on earth. Just find, as authentically as you can, what will give you joy and you'll reap the benefits in enjoying the "human" experience of finding it. Joy is in a banana split, a kiss, or a landscape of mountains and valleys.

> We are made to want and to desire. We are always creating, always building, always wanting for the good and better in our lives and the lives of those we love. It is the great sin of life not to want and not to desire. It is a heresy to think that we come to God (or some state of holiness) by killing our desire and our wanting. It just isn't the truth. Our wants and desires are not the source of our lives, nor the essence of what gives us satisfaction, but rather emerge from our being as an avenue to the Source beyond the things.

We are made to want and to desire. We are always creating, always building, always wanting for the good and better in our lives and the lives of those we love. It is the great sin of life not to want and not to desire. It is a heresy to think that we come to God (or some state of holiness) by killing our desire and our wanting. It just isn't the truth. Our wants and desires are not the source of our lives, nor the essence of what gives us satisfaction, but rather emerge from our being as an avenue to the Source beyond the things.

For example, I drive a Jaguar and I love it. I don't really love the car, I love the joy and enjoyment it gives me; I love the pleasure of driving that it gives. What I love is joy and pleasure, and I know that the Jaguar is not the source of that, but merely a vehicle to experiencing those states of mind. It is a wonderful tool and a wonderful way to these experiences.

Does it feed the starving children in the world? Maybe not directly, but it does provide a lot of jobs for a lot of good people. And yes, it is a contribution to my good and the good of other people. We feel far too guilty about these so-called attachments and luxuries of our lives. And Source or Universe or God or Higher Power gets to experience the ride in that Jag and what it's like for me when I drive it and enjoy it. My joy is often lived and experienced by those I love, who are on the receiving end. I live through those I love just like the Universe lives through me. Does the exhaust of the car pollute the world? Not as much as my joy cleans and purifies it, in the ongoing force and movement of creation. Joy creates. My joy creates and so does yours. And it creates a health that cleanses and purifies the world. Madonna sang that she was a "material girl" and mirrored the world, but I am not fooled that material treasures, while a beautiful emanation of one aspect of God or Source or Higher Power, are only a means to pleasure and joy which God experiences in my experiencing.

The problem occurs when we become attached to our wants and desires, to our "stuff" or things, as if they are THE Source, as if they are God. They are not God; they emanate from God as gifts from God and as the essence of that through which God continues to create. Be fundamentally attached to God or Universe or Source or Higher Power or whatever you call the divine substance that is the ground of your being, but love the desires and wants that emerge from that fundamental attachment to God. Just don't get them confused. Know what your Source is. Your Source is not your wants and desires; it is the one who creates them and fulfills them, and it is that ground of your being - that Source who lives and creates and experiences through the fulfillment of your wants and desires.

I am interested in hearing stories told by many conservative and fundamentalist believers claiming to be God's hands, God's feet, God's smile, etc., etc. But how about this? My taste buds are the way God experiences taste; my laughter is God experiencing and "feeling" laughter. Our human experience takes on a significant added dimension when we realize that when God created man and woman to soothe God's own loneliness, that Substance of all creation is still creating and still unfolding. God "feels" through us and knows delight and pleasure through us. If we consider that God is always experiencing through us, it might give us greater cause to more fully experience and enjoy the sex we have, the food we eat, and the nature of all our indulgences, which can be heightened because we are "seeing and feeling" the union that is God and the human experience. In the higher and higher levels of consciousness that affect our selectivity, detachment would likely be from things that express a lesser love of ourselves, rather than detachment for the sake of an obscurely understood and culturally misplaced spiritual value. Most people have given up on a great deal of what they want, detached long ago from their real wants and dreams. The treasured spiritual principle is in finding your wants, desires and passions and letting God experience creation through them. The spiritual journey is not "detachment". Indeed, it is a real attachment to what you love and long for and for having the courage to want it, and believing that is perfectly all right, so long as you do not harm another, in the pursuit of getting it. In the end, all of our wants and desires take us back to the deeper desires they serve as an avenue to fulfillment. The world expands and the universe and creation grows through your wanting and desiring. You don't have to explain them or feel guilty about them, either. They are creation unfolding through you; your desires and wants are to be enjoyed.

Let any *DownSpiral* you are in tell you what you want, but get into an *UpSpiral* as soon as possible. If you have trouble with this, go back to the *Emotional Gym* and the *UpSpiral* chapters. Live your strengths. Be your strengths. Make them reflexive in every situation in your life. They are as close to your real self as you can get.

Desires and wants emerge from using strengths. That's the answer to the first question, "How do I know what I want?" And by the way, it's OK on the journey to getting these wants and desires to change your mind. They aren't cast in stone. They are highly malleable. Let them morph and change and even alter your journey. They are by no means fixed.

How do you increase your "believing" was the second question. Believing also increases by being in the *UpSpiral* – it's a natural outcome of the *UpSpiral* for faith and sense of certitude to increase. It just happens that way. But believing increases most by being grateful and living in a state of appreciation. Gratitude creates the greatest changes in body chemistry and hormones. Hope is second. Love is third. You may have thought that love would be first. It's not. You don't love unless you have gratitude and hope. You are too shut down to love without gratitude and hope. Gratitude precedes all else, it is the opener of the sensory system. It is the great OK to life that tells the cells to function, thrive and metabolize. Lose your gratitude and you cut yourself off from life, both in body chemistry and hormones. Hope is second in producing the same changes in the body. Laugher in the healing process restores gratitude and hope - that's why it helps to laugh when you're trying to heal. It's a short cut to gratitude and hope.

Your Signature Strengths increase your believing. In your 10 Signature Strengths you will find the key to increasing your believing. You have, in your strengths, those that will return you to gratitude and hope. Find the strengths that are at your finger tips, that when you exercise them, increase your gratitude and your hope. As you do that, your strength in "believing" increases.

> Desires and wants emerge from using strengths. That's the answer to the first question, "How do I know what I want?" And by the way, it's OK on the journey to getting these wants and desires to change your mind. They aren't cast in stone. They are highly malleable. Let them morph and change and even alter your journey. They are by no means fixed.

The real evidence of the strength of your *VibeCore* is a state called flow. Just like there is objective research demonstrating that you can stay in an *UpSpiral*, there is research regarding how to stay in a state of flow. This is where the work of Dr. Mihaly Csikszentmihalyi (pronounced cheek-sent-me-high) is important. Several years ago, I picked up the Sunday **New York Times** to find on the cover one of the most hopeful articles I had read in psychology for a long time. The article and the research was prophetic, way back then, of the new emergence of the field of positive psychology. It was about a new book by Dr. Csikszentmihalyi about a state of mind or experience he had researched and named "flow". For Dr. C, as he is called by his students, flow is a state which can be measured and which is described as being "one with the music". I believe that what Dr. C describes is at the heart of what is our *VibeCore*. He describes a state he calls flow which is a somewhat altered state of consciousness that is easily attained. However, it's implications are highly significant.

At its essence, his work is some of the most significant research on how to increase our "believing", our "faith" and a sense of certitude and solidness about believing we can get what we want. It is a very subtle, but very significant by-product of the experience of flow. Extended experiences of flow, create a kind of faith and certitude that is so simple that it just "is". It creates the kind of easy believing and certitude that is so subtle it almost escapes both the participant and the observer. It is the experience from which "I know that I know what I know" occurs at a core level.

What does flow have to do with increasing faith? Flow is meditation in motion. It is the Zen of the Western world. It does for the brain, the psyche and the spirit what Zen and deep states of meditation do in more passive states of meditation. If traditional meditation is, for you, something like stopping a "diesel on a dime", then use flow as the meditation state of the active person, because that's exactly what it is. Flow is meditation.

What does flow have to do with increasing faith? Flow is meditation in motion. It is the Zen of the Western world. It does for the brain, the psyche and the spirit what Zen and deep states of meditation do in more passive states of meditation. If traditional meditation is, for you, something like stopping a "diesel on a dime", then use flow as the meditation state of the active person, because that's exactly what it is. Flow is meditation.

The experience of flow can be more important and more deeply significant than the emptying forms of meditation, because flow can teach us how to meditate all day long. Emptying forms of meditation, while helpful, are much more difficult to incorporate into daily activity. Simply put, Dr. C discovered, observed, and measured in his research that meditation is about the state of flow. The common components of the state of flow he has identified are:

- The goals are clear
- Feedback is immediate
- There is a balance between challenge and skill

- Concentration deepens
- The present is what matters
- Control is no problem
- The sense of time is altered
- There is a loss of ego

The research on the state of flow reveals that when a challenge can be matched with our skills, we become highly engaged or involved. This state describes the synchronicity and the vibration discussed in a previous chapter. As we get involved in a challenging activity, we increase that involvement as we see we are succeeding at doing it. This increased concentration or involvement is created, in part, by an immediate feedback loop that lets us know how we are doing, then and there. The ego forgets to judge, in the sense of "you are doing a good or a bad job". *The anxiety, worry, and fear circuitry of the brain is shut down during flow.* The ego stops evaluating and judging and basically shuts off. As soon as the ego reasserts itself, the experience is lost in the wrong kind of critical, or self-aware, evaluation. You have to be more lost in the process because this is precisely the place from which a more focused concentration for flow occurs. Concentration gets focused because of the challenge, our interest in the challenge and our success at meeting it. This activity which balances challenge and skills is pleasurable for the brain and it sidesteps the ego. You then get lost in the task and time flows effortlessly and unnoticed.

Dr. C believes that this activity of flow builds "psychological capital". This psychological capital is an increase in the capacity for believing, or faith. Faith is really a measure of the power of thought and not an ethereal religious concept. In the Bible, St. Paul says that faith is the hope of things unseen, knowing that what is not seen will be seen. This is the creative faith of the person in flow–that which is being created or done in the creative experience will "become". This is also not unlike the buffer zone of the *UpSpiral*.

Psychological capital is a strength of the neuronal inter-associations of the brain. Your brain makes more connections between the synapses, and as it does it is strengthened. In effect, it broadens and builds. *Your brain believes better, hopes more and creates with a "knowing" that is thought in motion.* The repertoire of the ideas, thoughts, and creativity is increased. This is the stuff that invents and builds new worlds. One new idea builds creatively upon another. It is important to realize that all of your neurons are a few acquaintances away from each other. That is to say, your neurons are only a few neurons away from vast associations with all neurons. It is like the studies showing that we are only three people removed from knowing anyone else in the United States and seven people removed from knowing anyone in the world.

Your brain in flow is revitalizing and renewing. It represents a state in which it operates most like its natural state – in a high degree of synchrony. This flow is meditation in motion; it is contemplation on the move. Many people who are not good at passive, emptying meditation practices will find that flow is a welcome, much more easily attained state of meditation and a relief from the daily spiritual practices they miss and feel guilty about. Flow is actually the experience that many people using drugs and alcohol or other means are trying to find or replicate but cannot.

Your brain in flow is revitalizing and renewing. It represents a state in which it operates most like its natural state – in a high degree of synchrony. This flow is meditation in motion; it is contemplation on the move. Many people who are not good at passive, emptying meditation practices will find that flow is a welcome, much more easily attained state of meditation and a relief from the daily spiritual practices they miss and feel guilty about.

Flow, in part can be described as losing yourself in something that is a challenge and "becoming one with the music", or one with the activity. This is the unitive state described in meditation and contemplation for men and women in the monastery of the world. However, as a measurable state, this is only a part of the picture of flow. This sense of flow is significant because it allows us to study flow from a scientific perspective. This notion of flow can belong to all of life. It is not absolutely essential that there be a challenge that matches our skills in the absolute sense of a single task or endeavor. The nature of challenge and skills in any area can vary, as it does in this match between knowing what you want and believing you will get it. As we previously discussed, that is called your *VibeCore*. We will see that the stronger your *VibeCore*, the greater your capacity to turn your life into flow.

Let me give a personal example. I had a cousin named Peter who owned a fish market, where I volunteered my services to help him out during a hard time. My first job was to clean the slime off of five bushels of clams. Not much fun. Nor was it very creative or interesting. It was Peter's idea of an initiation, I reasoned. It was certainly not a challenge. Or was it? I thought to myself: Here I am with a Yale degree and doctorate from Harvard cleaning clams. But I want to help my cousin, even if this dinky, dingy, hole in the wall fish market does seem to be a bit beneath me. Actually it was one of those places that are a "find". The food was great, the atmosphere could not have been replicated by the best designer and it just was one of those places that worked. Had it been next to a college campus, it would have been "the place to go", but stuck in a working class neighborhood, it was just part of the landscape and entirely taken for granted. And therein is the challenge. How do I take the ordinary, mundane, stinky, boring, ho-hum task, and make it a challenge, a bit of a flow activity? ***And that is the issue with flow.*** Anything in life can be seen in the light of the challenge to use one's strengths - the wide spectrum of them, to be in flow. *In fact, to see life as the challenge and to respond with one's skills in order to stay in a state of flow is the start of the trick to doing this.* It is at the heart of your *VibeCore*. All of life can be a flow if the challenge is to remain in that vibrational state, no matter what. If I can do it with five bushels of clams, you can do it with anything in your life. In fact, that was the gift the slime and the clams gave to me. All of life can be a flow. I just happened to learn this vital truth in a simple, humble little fish market from the willingness, in an act of love, to help a cousin. In fact, if we learn to do this in the slime of life and wherever we might find ourselves, we will be able to apply it to all of life.

Let me tell you how I did it with the clams and soon you'll be writing me to tell me how you're doing it with not only the "slime" in your life, but with loveliest and the greatest challenges as well. These are the experiences of life that build your *VibeCore*. Take the challenge in front of you, make it a flow, and in the process let it help you define what you want and know you can get it. Make whatever it is give you its secrets of self-revelation.

As I took each clam, I focused only on the clam, the water, the cleaning brush and the experience. Anytime my thoughts strayed anywhere else I said, "Just this" and I returned to focus on the clams. I returned my focus to the task of cleaning the clams each time my mind went to something else. I didn't have a chance to ask, how was I doing, how many were left or when would I be finished (the ego interrupting). I just focused and dismissed every thought with "just this". I was finished with five bushels of clams before I knew it, and I was relaxed. The process went easily and smoothly. The time flew by and I was never bored or disinterested. "Just this" kept my mind focused and I just flowed with the experience. I also did not evaluate my experience. I didn't ask whether this was a waste of my time. I just did it. I became "one with the clams" and the time whizzed by. Not only that, but it was relaxing, I let go, I didn't compare. I didn't measure except to know that each clam was clean. I did, however, change my approach as I went along. I was always open to new and better ways of doing the cleaning as the process went on. I learned how to position the clams differently, how to move them more efficiently and how best to place them in the bushel. I even became more dexterous with the brush. There was a constant feedback loop that was telling me how well I was doing and how I could improve to make the process more efficient. This feedback loop is always a part of flow. In this case, the challenge may have been far beneath my intellectual skills, but it indeed was a challenge and I could get better at how I busheled the clams. Interestingly enough, the required focus on the clams was no different a discipline than had I been silently tucked away meditating on only my breathing. The only difference was that there were five bushels of cleaned clams when I was finished.

The interesting thing was my attitude. I enjoyed doing the job; it wasn't tedious and it wasn't unpleasant. It "just was" and I enjoyed the feeling of accomplishing the task. Never sell short the sense of accomplishment that comes from doing even the most menial task well. It is part of the work ethic that seems to get easily lost today.

I then went on to transfer this ability to get into flow, from clams to installing ceiling fans. We decided that we wanted ceiling fans in five rooms of our home. I decided to put them up and to make doing so a flow activity. This was considerably more difficult because I had never installed ceiling fans before and the wiring in the house was old. However, in this situation, I faced the possibility of failure: maybe I didn't have the ability to figure out how to install the fans and maybe I would not do it correctly. The ceiling lights had to work independently from a fan that had to turn at three speeds. While I believed that I could meet this challenge, I was not at all sure. But I wanted five ceiling fans in my house and I believed I could do it - I just didn't know then that this was my *VibeCore* at work.

So after I got started, every time I became worried that I would be unable to do the job, I said "just this" and focused in on the task. Remember the various steps of flow. This was certainly a challenge for which I might or might not have the skills. There was a feedback loop, so I could see how I was doing. Again, though, something that might have been taxing, boring or just plain frustrating was not allowed to be so. It became flow largely because when these feelings might have set in, I managed my focus and said, "just this". For example, the directions were poor and had some pictures with poor descriptions. Instead of fear, I said "just this" and studied the directions until I understood them. There were times when I would encounter a problem or run into a snag that made me think I wasn't doing well (the ego evaluating and breaking focus), but I would say "just this" and go back to concentrating on how to get the job done. Before long the first fan was up and when I flipped the switch and the fan started going around, it was almost bliss. When I flipped the other switch and the lights also went on, it was for sure bliss. Well, if not bliss, I felt a great deal of self-satisfaction and a sense of fulfillment. A day later, all of the fans were spinning around and the lights were working correctly, too. I could easily have spent my time with my legs folded and doing "just this" and focusing on my breathing, and there is certainly a place for that. But I am a Western man in a material world and the diesel of my drive does not stop easily on a dime. I did the "ceiling fan" meditation, and as I did my spirit was as peaceful as the gentle breeze of the ceiling fan on low and glowed like the lighting fixture.

Anything can be a flow activity with the right state of mind, not necessarily because it has to be an absolute match of challenge and skill. The challenge can be the job itself or the challenge can be just the focus. The challenge can be anything you want. I do the same thing now, whenever I have to clean. It is a "just this" exercise. Whenever I have to do something that is not particularly pleasant or something I might not want to do, I can turn it into a "just this" experience of flow. But more importantly, I have realized it represents a vibration that is my *VibeCore* and it has grown to much larger and greater life "wantings".

This larger experience that is flow, and the growing sense of this vibration that is the *VibeCore*, however, isn't just the experience of being "one with" the activity. It isn't just that I can make any activity into a kind of meditation. It is a certain competence in managing thinking and feeling while matching it with believing, that is the flow. I can "want" to get the activity done, and I am matching that with the belief that I can do it by turning it into a flow activity that is good for me. That is both a challenge and a match of want and belief. The match of wanting and believing, this *VibeCore*, can be flow whenever you are precise about what you want and believe you can have, get, or do it. This is the energy of the vibration that we are.

It is interesting to consider procrastination here. It is a small example of the nature of the *VibeCore*. In fact, it's the opposite of your *VibeCore* being in place. Procrastination is a sign that wanting or believing (or both) are not matched to a high enough, or clear enough degree, to proceed. Considering procrastination makes the notion of one's *VibeCore* more real and tangible. Procrastination is simply a sign that it is not the time to do that activity, if at all. There are those who would argue that the best way to get over procrastination is just to do the thing. However, even if doing it gets you motivated, doing it is behavior that has changed either the wanting or the believing that you could get it done. Just getting the task done may work for simple or small cases of procrastination, but larger issues of procrastination will not be solved just by taking action or by getting the "doing" going. It is deeper than that. It is about finding your wanting and your believing. It's about getting your *VibeCore* set so the vibration is right and all the energy you need, will be right there. Procrastination, in the larger issues of life is, about knowing what it is you really want; wanting it and believing you can do it. When it comes to larger things you are procrastinating about, it is about getting these two things straight, so your *VibeCore* is high and your energy to do it will just be there. The absence of energy of the *VibeCore* is about the lack of the match between wanting and believing. Procrastination is a sign that you are not ready to move ahead. Your energy is not aligned. Therefore, you will have a very difficult time bringing into your life what you want and getting done what you want to get accomplished. Listen to the procrastination and see what messages it has to tell you about what you really want and what you really believe. Find out what you really believe about an activity you procrastinate doing and you will likely find out that your motivation to do it is low because you really don't want it. It likely has little to do with being lazy or unmotivated as much as going in the wrong direction or doing it at the wrong time.

The experience of the *VibeCore* and flow has so far been about a state of mind that describes a kind of "going with the flow", "one with the music" sort of existence. It is one that we can have most of the time. It is not so much a match between challenge and skills, but instead is a match between "wants and beliefs". It is not struggling. It is going with the flow of life. It is a vibration.

StrengthSmart and the *VibeCore*

Being "*StrengthSmart*" has a great deal to do with *VibeCore*. In the activities with the clams and the ceiling fans, I was aware of using my strengths, of referencing them and plugging them into what I was doing. They were part of both my motivation and inspiration base. By being mindful of my strengths and drawing on them or playing to them, I was not allowing into my awareness my weaknesses that are great distracters of being able to get anything done. For example, one of my strengths is the appreciation of beauty and excellence. The clams, their shapes, textures, and their lines were like fingerprints. The colors of blue to gray and back to lines of white were beautiful. You may think this is insignificant, but this use of strengths is enough to create a shift in consciousness, from not being interested in something to being increasingly captivated by it. It is a doorway to creativity. One of my strengths is "maximizer". That means I draw out the best in a situation. I was challenged to make this the most productive time it could be. I also wanted to maximize the effectiveness of my friend's fish market. Zest and enthusiasm are strengths and are a ready friend. Why not be enthusiastic over clams? That would certainly pull on and grow strength. Why complain and feel negative? There's the choice and enthusiasm is my strength, right at my finger tips, so why not use it? Bravery, courage and valor are another of my strengths. What does it take to clean clams? Bravery and courage? No. But valor, yes. It did take some valor. I was there to help; it was a good and right thing to do. What is important about this is that whether it's cleaning clams or living life, we have strengths readily at our disposal. When we exercise the choice to use them, we can master most any situation and turn it into flow. Your Signature Strengths are always sufficient in any situation to shift your consciousness to creating a *VibeCore* in yourself to meet the task at hand or to let you know that you have no business doing what you're doing and you need to change your direction.

By the time you are working on the material in *VibeCore*, you need to have become at least somewhat reflexive with your strengths. Be used to using them and getting into a flow will be much easier.

VibeCore is the place of your basic movement into and attach-

ment to the world. It is the place from which you either "go for it"
or you don't.

What you want may change in the process of bringing it into your
life. It may change in nature, and it may come in a different package than you expected, but it will come. What is the proof of this?
Is there a proof? Yes. There are two places; the first is not as important as the second. The first is research and the second is your history. Since your history is the most important, let's look at that first.

How do I come to believe that I'm going to get it? I mean, really
believe it?

If you look at your history and you are honest, the proof is there.
If you look at your history and you have shed the skin of the past,
so you are not looking like or sounding like a "victim", the proof is
definitely there. If you aren't feeling sorry for yourself and if you're
honestly assessing where you are in life, you will find that you have
gotten pretty much everything you have wanted in one way or
another. Where one door may have closed another door opened.
Because you are born with resilience, "bounce back", and an enormous capacity to process and learn from what has happened to you,
in such a way, that always, where one door has closed, another has
opened. It has brought, often disguised, what you really wanted.
Maybe all that you wanted isn't here, but what you wanted is largely what you have gotten.

You may not have liked everything you got. You may have
changed your mind about it when you got it, but all it did was form
the next desire, the next want, and then you went on to get that in
some form or another. It is also true, if you are honest with yourself,
that what you have resented and been angry about for a long time or
whined about forever, has resulted in you creating more of the same
in your life. Maybe you don't like what you got, but you got what
you wanted and it tried to teach you how to want with more clarity
and self-understanding. What we are getting now is still trying to

teach us these lessons. If you see what you have gotten - whatever it may be - as a gift, that it is always a gift and are willing to learn the lessons it teaches, then you will get what you want faster and the next door will open more quickly. Actually, the next doors open very quickly, usually. This whole process of life has been in the process of strengthening your *VibeCore*, if you are honest about it. We do not spend nearly as much time as we think wandering in dark hallways unless we choose to. To sustain addictions, we really don't want new doors to open. We'd rather escape instead.

Try this exercise. Make a list of every door that you feel has been closed in your life. Then make a list of every door that opened. You will find that, tit for tat, one door closed and another door opened. Or you will find that when one door opened and you walked through, gratefully or not, that another door opened. If you walked through the door in gratitude, the next door probably opened easier and better, because that's what you helped to create. We are enormous creators of our own lives. We are enormous magnets that draw to us what matches our *VibeCore*.

> This whole process of life has been in the process of strengthening your *VibeCore*, if you are honest about it. We do not spend nearly as much time as we think wandering in dark hallways unless we choose to. To sustain addictions, we really don't want new doors to open. We'd rather escape instead.

It is hard to be this honest. But if you are, you have found that the greater responsibility you take for having largely created your own life, the more freedom you have and the greater your sense of your own power. The greatest proof of your *VibeCore* and its power in your life is finding its truth in your history.

If you are honest, you will conclude that you have brought into your life, by the match of your wanting and believing, most everything you wanted. That doesn't mean that you have liked it – it just means that you have created it. It is a matter of what we choose to make of the difficulty or to not make of the difficulty that is important. The degree to which you know what your *VibeCore* is and that it is indeed you, will lead to the greatest thing you have going for you, for the rest of your life.

Some of the strongest research in this area was initially done by Dr. Martin Seligman and discussed in his book **Learned Optimism**. The book provides a broad underlining of the difference between optimism and pessimism and the effects of each.

For further evidence do an internet search on Google. There are pages and pages of research studies and articles measuring the relationship between belief and outcome. Try entering "research on belief and outcome" or "motivation, belief, and outcome" or "belief and motivation", varying the themes and you will find more research than you could read in a lifetime. Why then do we have such questions about whether or not we attract what we believe? We already know that we attract what we believe and we already know that we create it on every level of the human experience. We already know the importance of wanting, belief and motivation. The results are there. What then, is in the way? Why have we just not done it?

If you are honest, you will conclude that you have brought into your life, by the match of your wanting and believing, most everything you wanted. That doesn't mean that you have liked it – it just means that you have created it. It is a matter of what we choose to make of the difficulty or to not make of the difficulty that is important. The degree to which you know what your *VibeCore* is and that it is indeed you, will lead to the greatest thing you have going for you, for the rest of your life.

The answer is relatively simple. Ways of thinking kept the dark ages in the dark and then came enormous breakthroughs. It is the same today. Our "dark age" has been our focus on the problem or on the illness, doing therapy and finding cures for mental illness and mental health issues. What we call mental health is really about mental illness. We have believed that our unconscious mind or factors beyond our control most affected our successful outcomes. This simply isn't true. We have only, in the last 10 years, started to focus on what works, not what needs to be healed. We have only started to focus on the nature of the *UpSpiral* rather than curing the *DownSpiral*. We have only recently begun to be interested in focusing on strengths and growing them rather than focusing entirely on weaknesses and changing them. We have not applied the research we have, because it has not been favored by granting agencies or what has been taught in our universities. Religion has kept us almost entirely focused on sin and what is wrong with us. Westerners are haunted by doctrines like "original sin" yet many of those who have given up the idea of sin have sold out only to be haunted by a fundamentalist understanding of their "karma" that will catch up with them. Where religion hasn't had this focus on the negative, business has taken up with evaluations to create "well-rounded employees" who work on and overcome their deficits. For the most part, cultural focus has been on fixing what is wrong, rather than growing what is right, strong, and good, when it comes to human beings. Being positive has been seen as Pollyanna and being negative has been seen as being critical, intelligent, and reasoned. Being positive has been seen as being unrealistic. Fortunately that is changing.

Could it really be as easy as growing what is good? Yes, it is as easy as that. It is also more effective and it produces more lasting results.

Everybody has a *VibeCore*. It is as palpable as your heartbeat. We talk about each other's "vibes"; we are sensitive to people who are vibrating at a level lower than ours and know that they bring us down. We are also sensitive to people who vibrate at a higher level than we do. They bring us up, or if not, they challenge – or at least intimidate or awe us. You have a *VibeCore*. You not only have this core but you grow it. You can make your vibration stronger, bigger and better. In doing so you will - I promise - get more of what you want. You will likely get it quicker and you will get more of it than you expected.

All of the exercises in this book are about growing your *VibeCore*. If you grow the positive mind, the *UpSpiral*, you will inevitably grow your *VibeCore*. You can't grow in an *UpSpiral* and not do it. It really is the key to everything. Feel better, get to feeling good, stay there awhile and all aspects of your life will improve. Stay in an *UpSpiral* and you will intuitively become *StrengthSmart*. Stay in an *UpSpiral* and you will increase your *VibeCore*. Stay in an *UpSpiral* and you will define your FuturePac. Stay in an *UpSpiral* and you will find your vision. Stay in an *UpSpiral* and revelation will be yours. The key is feeling good in the *UpSpiral*. It is not any more difficult than that. These additional steps just help you do it better, faster, and with a greater sense of certainty.

Think of your *VibeCore* as where you are essentially, most internally, coming from. It is the essence of you, expressed in a vibration of energy created and exuded by you, attracting like energy to you. A hint about how powerful your *VibeCore* is may be found in an important memory. Think of a time when you were at your very best, a specific time when you were at your peak performance. That time was characterized by a high degree of focus on what you wanted and the fact that you believed you would get it. That memory of you at your best is a memory of you being determined to do or be something, coupled with a sense of certainty that you could and would. There may well have been some risk involved but this match of wanting and believing pushed you beyond the risk and into you being at your best. You can reclaim that moment and you can live your life with that degree of decision and power.

Everybody has a *VibeCore*. It is as palpable as your heartbeat. We talk about each other's "vibes"; we are sensitive to people who are vibrating at a level lower than ours and know that they bring us down. We are also sensitive to people who vibrate at a higher level than we do. They bring us up, or if not, they challenge – or at least intimidate or awe us. You have a *VibeCore*. You not only have this core but you grow it. You can make your vibration stronger, bigger and better. In doing so; you will - I promise - get more of what you want. You will likely get it quicker and you will get more of it than you expected.

Let's review where we are so far. The state of mind which is flow or vibration is the match between what you want and what you believe in. It is an attractor or a magnetic state. It is a state of mind, grounded in a particular way of believing that gets you basically, in one way or another, what you want. Learn to stay in flow, knowing what you want and believing that you're going to get it. Where one door may have closed, another has opened. The truth of the matter is, the closed door is probably much more important than the one that opened, because it pointed the way and gave the energy for the next to open, so it goes all the way through life. Let any door that has closed make you face up to and clarify what you want. Define what you want. Give it greater and greater clarity.

VibeCore is your way of matching challenges and skills. Your *VibeCore* is what is essentially attracting to you what you want. But the essence of the greatest power of your *VibeCore* is this: If you look at your history and see for yourself that you have already gotten pretty much of everything that you ever wanted or that it has always worked out predominantly in that direction, then you are ready for the next step. You believe that everything you want is, more or less, already there; it's just waiting for you. You have, in effect, won the PowerBall Lottery of the Universe. It's done. It's waiting for you. All you have to do is live in a flow, matching your wants and your beliefs, seeing your challenges and matching them with your strengths and you've got it all. Just imagine for a minute how you would feel and what you would be like if you knew that you won the PowerBall lottery. After the initial excitement, how would you feel? My guess is that you would feel relieved, confident, peaceful, assured, quieted, serene, etc. Now just borrow that set of feelings and reactions to that imaginary scene and apply it to what you want. You already have the history that you're going to get it one way or another. Now apply the feelings and the sense of it to what you want for the rest of your life. Now act like that's true and live like that's true. Act! Fake it till you make it. Believe it and live it, because, one way or another, it is true, based on your past. Feel in the essence of your *VibeCore*, this moment, how you would feel if you already had it all. Live with the internal vibration that what you want is what you have already received. We tell addicts, when they are feeling down and tempted to give into the addiction, fake it till you make it. You do the same - fake it, act like you already have everything you're wanting, until you believe that you do. As you cross over this thin line from acting "as if" to walking into that space of really knowing, you will soon have it all. ***The secret of the VibeCore is to feel and live like you got it before it seems to show up.*** However, this is not a fake feeling or act. It just means using "fake it till you make it", or whatever strategy works for you, to get to the place where you are in the state of mind that appreciates, sees and knows, from your present perspective. Then it shows up.

How do I stay open to the variety of ways this can come into my life and to the variety of ways I can create it and that it can come to me?

Start to watch the circumstances in your life. The signs will come. There will be an article here or a chance meeting there, and odd occurrences of events that start to happen in a sequence and you will know that something is trying to be revealed. Sooner or later, you will know, in your heart of hearts, where it really matters, what only you can know for you, and that is that your *VibeCore* creates your life. What you believe and what you want creates your life.

There is a *VibeCore* Scale inside of you and you're on it, somewhere. Let's review. That *VibeCore* is your vibration. It is your flow in the world and it can get you what you want if you learn to really want it and decide to do so. On a scale of 1 -100, one is not knowing what you want nor being able to believe that you'll get it and 100 is knowing precisely what you want and being very certain that you will get it. You are always somewhere on this scale in every area of your life. There is an intensity to our vibration – to this match between our wanting and our believing. There is a number you can subjectively give yourself that represents how much you know that you want what you want. If I ask you to give a number that relates to the strength of knowing what you want, you could come up with a subjective digit of how much you know the strength or intensity of that wanting is. That subjective number would, across the board, be a pretty correct indicator of whether or not you will bring it into your life. It is also an indicator of how much flow you will experience in bringing it into your life. It is a measure of how much you will struggle and work at it and how much it will just be a flow that you welcomed and created in your life.

Remember, you bring into your life pretty much what you desire, as you increase your score up the Vibe Scale. You bring whatever it is you want more effortlessly the higher your score is. People, particularly those in an *UpSpiral*, are very good at assessing the strength of their own wanting. What is the strength of your own knowing what you want, on a scale of 1-100? How clear are you and how consistent are you with this wanting? How detailed are you in the wanting? How colorfully can you paint a picture with your imagination in your mind of what you want in many different areas on many different levels? What is your number today on a scale of 1 to 100?

> That *VibeCore* is your vibration. It is your flow in the world and it can get you what you want if you learn to really want it and decide to do so.

Now do the same thing with what you "believe". If 1 is not believing anything good could happen to you, just despair and despondency and 100 is being certain that you will get what you want, where would you subjectively score yourself?

Now do the same with the third measure of the *VibeCore* which is "openness" or "letting go". A "1" means that you are tightly holding on to the way you think everything happens, full of control, with an airtight hold on what it is, how it has to happen, and when. 100 is letting whatever it is happen in its own time, in whatever package it shows up in, out of your absolute control and open to all of the surprises of how what you want can come to you.

Subjectively add these scores together in your mind and get a "sort of" score of where you are. You will know which area is your weakness. If you absolutely have to you can break them down and analyze where you are, but use this as a general sort of measure of the inner vibration of your *VibeCore*.

Now look at these numbers. How high are they? How do they match? The core of your vibration in life is both the strength of these numbers and the degree to which they match. You will bring them into your life on the basis of the match. The strength of the match describes how you will bring them to you. There is a hitch to this and here it is. It is not entirely a matter of the strength of your *VibeCore*. It is also a matter of getting going and keeping it going in an ascending and increasingly positive direction. To be a magnet for what you want in life, you don't have to be a 100. You just have to be headed in that direction. Keep pointed in the right direction and the energy of the *UpSpiral* will take you along.

The stronger your *VibeCore*, the clearer your vibration, the greater your flow will bring into your life what you really want. The higher the *VibeCore*, the more effortlessly you will do this in a flow and the quicker and easier it will happen for you. People with lower *VibeCore*s get what they want, but they try harder and they struggle longer and they create more drama in the process. Your certitude is predictive of the flow and of letting it happen. When we later set goals to this wanting, there will be action steps, but they will still be characterized by a flow based in assurance and certitude. People with a higher *VibeCore* are more in a flow of matching wanting, believing, and being open. It seems to "just happen" more for them because they aren't trying so hard and getting in their own way.

This is your *VibeCore*. And from that essence you start to build on what you want, to claim it, to know it, and to own it. And you can claim what you want without fear, shame or guilt and without giving a hoot what anybody else thinks about what you want, so long as what you want doesn't harm anyone else. From there you start believing that you will get it. The more you do this and the more you follow the suggestions in this book, the more you will grow into a state of mind I call certitude.

I have a song that I play when I want to feel certitude - when I want to get into that state of mind. It puts me there every time, right on time. And I have to listen to a particular singer sing it. It is **Close Every Door** from Andrew Lloyd Weber's Broadway production of

Joseph's Amazing Technicolor Dream Coat and it is sung by Donny Osmond. After I had adopted this song and Osmond's rendition of it as my certitude song, I happened to meet the first "Joseph" from the play on Broadway. He told me about being the youngest member ever in the cast and playing this role until the production started to really roll and they wanted star power. This young man helped to train Donny Osmond to sing the song. He described Osmond as being completely open and willing to learn, easy to work with, and appreciative of everything Trini had to teach him. I can tell you one thing. When Donny Osmond sings this song, he understands what he is singing about. He has what this song is about in his heart and he passes it on to me and, I'm sure, a large number of other people whose lives he's touched.

The song, **"Close Every Door"** is about Joseph, imprisoned and seemingly lost and abandoned and he sings this incredible song. Essentially the meaning of the song is to "take everything from me - my name, my friends, my family - every aspect of my identity that you think you can take but there is one thing that you cannot take from me. Ever. It is the certain knowledge that I have been promised a land of my own and I will get it.

The song and the play is not about a specific piece of land. Instead it is about the promised land that is within each of us. We will know and possess this interior land that is our own heart and self and this "land of my own" will be the fulfillment of the person I am, living in love, in the world. Andrew Lloyd Weber knows what he is writing about. He knows and understands this search - that each of us has to claim our own inner promised land and Osmond sings it perfectly, knowing it as well.

Knowing what you want, believing you will get it, and a certain kind of letting go is flow in life.

This is one of the songs that I use in my *Emotional Gym* whenever I want to feel a sense of certitude immediately, for a duration of time, and intensely. I practice feeling certitude with this music.

It is this certitude that is your *VibeCore* within you. It is knowing what you want and believing that you will get it. When you do, what will come out of you is a vibration that will attract to you the essence and fullness of your real self and all that you want to fill in your own promised land.

Your *VibeCore* is your point of certitude. Continue to strengthen it by considering your *FuturePac,* explained in the next chapter, which will help fill in the details that will take you further on the journey.

Knowing what you want, believing you will get it, and a certain kind of letting go is flow in life.

Workout #4: *Emotional Gym* for *VibeCore*

The previous exercises have helped you build **immediacy**. You are now able to get to any of the five emotions with great immediacy, if not instantly, and upon call. They are at your finger tips. Continue to do those exercises.

Now we begin to work on the duration and the intensity of these emotions.

Find five songs that arouse in you the five emotions of gratitude, love, peace, hope, and joy. They need to be five different songs, one for each emotion.

Play the songs at different times during the day, but try to start your day with your gratitude song. If you can do it, use each song every day. If not, scatter and vary them throughout the week. Be sure to feel the emotion you are attaching to the song, throughout the song. If you forget and think about something else, just go easily back to the emotion. Also, as you draw the emotion out (duration) also increase how much you feel the feeling. In other words, increase the intensity of the emotion. Let it last. Let it build and let it grow. You are building your reservoir of positive emotion and the strengths of your buffer zone.

VibeCore Summary

The higher your *VibeScore*, the stronger and fuller is your positive mind. It relates to whether you draw people to you, leave them where they are, or repel them away from you. Your 'vibe" plugs you into certain situations and it leads you away from others. Your *VibeCore* is kind of like your inner magnet. It defines what you will bring into your life, what you will allow in. It also defines the "vibe" you are putting out. It is like an electro magnet. The greater the electrical energy that flows through the magnet, the stronger its pull.

We are made to want and to desire. We are always creating, always building, always wanting for the good and better in our lives and the lives of those we love. It is the great sin of life not to want and not to desire. It is a heresy to think that we come to God (or some state of holiness) by killing our desire and our wanting. It just isn't the truth. Our wants and desires are not the source of our lives, nor the essence of what gives us satisfaction, but rather emerge from our being as an avenue to the Source beyond the things.

Desires and wants emerge from using strengths. That's the answer to the first question, "How do I know what I want?" And by the way, it's OK on the journey to getting these wants and desires to change your mind. They aren't cast in stone. They are highly malleable. Let them morph and change and even alter your journey. They are by no means fixed.

What does flow have to do with increasing faith? Flow is meditation in motion. It is the Zen of the Western world. It does for the brain, the psyche and the spirit what Zen and deep states of meditation do in more passive states of meditation. If traditional meditation is, for you, something like stopping a "diesel on a dime", then use flow as the meditation state of the active person, because that's exactly what it is. Flow is meditation.

Your brain in flow is revitalizing and renewing. It represents a state in which it operates most like its natural state – in a high degree of synchrony. This flow is meditation in motion; it is contemplation on the move. Many people who are not good at passive, emptying meditation practices will find that flow is a welcome, much more easily attained state of meditation and a relief from the daily spiritual practices they miss and feel guilty about.

This whole process of life has been in the process of strengthening your *VibeCore*, if you are honest about it. We do not spend nearly as much time as we think wandering in dark hallways unless we choose to. To sustain addictions, we really don't want new doors to open. We'd rather escape instead.

If you are honest, you will conclude that you have brought into your life, by the match of your wanting and believing, most everything you wanted. That doesn't mean that you have liked it – it just means that you have created it. It is a matter of what we choose to make of the difficulty or to not make of the difficulty that is important. The degree to which you know what your *VibeCore* is and that it is indeed you, will lead to the greatest thing you have going for you, for the rest of your life.

Everybody has a *VibeCore*. It is as palpable as your heartbeat. We talk about each other's "vibes"; we are sensitive to people who are vibrating at a level lower than ours and know that they bring us down. We are also sensitive to people who vibrate at a higher level than we do. They bring us up, or if not, they challenge – or at least intimidate or awe us. You have a *VibeCore*. You not only have this core but you grow it. You can make your vibration stronger, bigger and better. In doing so; you will - I promise - get more of what you want. You will likely get it quicker and you will get more of it than you expected.

That *VibeCore* is your vibration. It is your flow in the world and it can get you what you want if you learn to really want it and decide to do so.

Knowing what you want, believing you will get it, and a certain kind of letting go is flow in life.

FuturePac

Follow the directions in this chapter and you will emerge with a sense of vision and direction for your life

Your brain is a highly efficient organism. The move, motion or tendency of it is toward synchronicity, harmony, rhythm, and flow. We even organize a description of the brain at work and describe four patterns of harmony and synchronicity; alpha, beta, delta, and theta. But synchronicity is the best description. Working toward an economy of energy, always, the brain is synchronous and seeks a harmony. It does this by a general movement in the organization of function and information by moving from generalization to specificity. The brain seeks specificity. Your brain has an enormous capacity to intake information and to sort and store it in an orderly way, which is phenomenally astounding. But, the motion of your brain is always toward synchronization and specificity. Your brain wants to be specific, and then to go to higher levels. Once specific, it generalizes again, always seeking higher and higher levels of generalization and then onto specificity again.

If you have the idea that setting goals is limiting and that it is better to just let things unfold, you aren't going to like this chapter. In fact, you may not even like this book. This is a book about things unfolding, but only after things have been brought to specificity. The operative word is "decision". You are being moved to decision. Decisions mark an end point of the input of data into the brain. Then the brain works with those decisions; it grows from them, collecting information that supports these decisions or information that these decisions need to be altered.

One of the reasons for great angst of indecision is a brain signaling for synchronicity and less use of psychic energy. We are, indeed, living in a time of great indecision. Bombarded by too much negative information, confronted with an overload of choices and a rapidly-changing technology of delivery systems, indecision is a malaise of our times, and the condition is increasing. Indecision causes your brain great unrest.

The move of your brain toward specificity happens so that unfolding can occur. But if you want to be diffuse and "just let things unfold", this will not work for you. If you want unfolding, you will get unfolding. The brain will unfold and meander. It will wander and it will be diffuse, but it will use more psychic energy in organizing and learning and will act with less synchronicity. In short, it will be difficult for your brain to move forward. The right hemisphere is charged with getting the "whole picture" and the left frontal lobe is charged with direction and vision. Interrupt that synchronicity and you get diffusion, difficulty with consistent perspective and what appears as directionlessness. The brain has to organize itself and learn from that organization to move forward. If you want outcomes and results, and enormous unfolding along the way of being specific, then you will do fine. This is because you will be working in coordination with your brain. Your brain will just unfold for you all over the place, but it will not be a happy brain. It will be over-taxed in unproductive ways and you will likely experience too many highs and lows. Happy brains move from generalities to specificity or synchronization.

One of the reasons for great angst of indecision is a brain signaling for synchronicity and less use of psychic energy. We are, indeed, living in a time of great indecision. Bombarded by too much negative information, confronted with an overload of choices and a rapidly-changing technology of delivery systems, indecision is a malaise of our times, and the condition is increasing. Indecision causes your brain great unrest.

This chapter is about building a *FuturePac,* which is a collection of six five-year goals that are highly planned, but highly malleable. It is about growing your brain and growing you. These goals can change at any time, based on the feedback you are getting about them. However, when they become goals, they will, at that time, be the best reflection of what you want - what you really want - that you can bring together. When you have identified these goals you will have a sense of knowing where you're at and where you're going. It is a wonderful sense of direction leading to confidence and relief. The specifics of the goals may change, but the sense of direction will remain and provide a sense of wholeness, as well. As long as you are working toward these goals in both general and concrete actions that are in a flow, you are going to experience aliveness, excitement, and anticipation.

The purpose of the *FuturePac* is to move you toward your vision and passion in life, and that will become your *MasteRevelation*, the revealing of meaning and significance in your life, as you define it. The *FuturePac*, then, is a step on the way to finding your vision for life, at any stage of life, wherever you are in life, no matter how lost or how found you may be.

You will or may have already found that after you have become *StrengthSmart* and that as your strengths have become reflexive, along with your growing *VibeCore*, more and more wants and desires have bubbled up. You are wanting more and knowing more of what you want. Your desires have increased and have greater specificity. You have new wants and desires and old ones have come more alive, even though some have been left behind. It is a natural thing for wants and desires to bubble forth when you use your strengths; they just create more wants and desires. It is this wanting and desiring that is ongoing creation, and it is the way you are part of making creation happen. The energy and vibration of your wanting and desiring puts stretch marks in the Universe. That is one of the things that our satellites in space have discovered - stretch marks - undeniable proof that the Universe is expanding. Your creative use of thought is connected with that expansion. Your increase in wanting and desiring is a part of that total increasing. Your wants and desires are essential to your life. You have to want and you have to desire and the more you know what you want and desire, the better off you are and will become.

Write down anything and everything you want on post-it notes –the sticky ones that you can put somewhere and move around. Start writing and writing every single want and desire on its own post-it note. It's important that each one gets its own post-it note. Next, randomly stick your post-it notes to the pages of a large scrapbook. Do not just make a list of your wants. You will need to move these thoughts around and sticky notes are the best way to do this.

> Write down anything and everything you want on post-it notes –the sticky ones that you can put somewhere and move around. Start writing and writing every single want and desire on its own post-it note.

As you dream and imagine and write them down and post them to your journal, think in even larger terms. You can even be silly and ridiculous. Make up some that seem silly and incomprehensible; it loosens you and your creative process up a bit. Put down some desires and wants that seem ridiculous and very far out of reach and just stick them in your book. The idea is, for a while, as you continue to do the exercises in the book, to write down as many of these ideas of wants and desires as you can. Later, in the sorting process, we will get rid of the ones that you don't want or no longer seem applicable. And you will find that once you have them written down and have formed them in your mind, some of them will happen even before you have time to organize them. Do not give any attention to "how" these things will happen. The "how" is not your business at this point.

> What you are doing is getting out of your mind and onto paper a thousand ideas, thoughts, wants and desires. It doesn't matter how little or big or petty or unrealistic each one seems. The key is to just get them all down.

What you are doing is getting out of your mind and onto paper a thousand ideas, thoughts, wants and desires. It doesn't matter how little or big or petty or unrealistic each one seems. The key is to just get them all down. There are 15 categories that you need to consider. I'd like to see you get about 20 wants and desires for each area. That sounds like a lot, but if you write down everything and get every want and desire out of you, you'll soon fill up your scrapbook. Whatever you put on a sticky note can easily be discarded at a later time because only one idea is on each note. But the more you write, the more ideas you will have and the more you will get in touch with what you really want. Later, in the sorting of these sticky notes, themes will begin to appear that will give greater clarity.

The 15 areas are:

- Professional (if you are retired, we still consider volunteer work professional as are ways in which you still think and work from your professional life, whether or not you are paid.)
- Financial
- Spiritual
- Physical
- Friends
- Family
- Intimacy
- Home and Environment
- Play and Fun
- Education/New Learning
- Adventure (even if you think you're too old for it, you're not, so put it down)
- Growth
- The Completely New and Novel
- New Learning
- Breaking Taboos
- Wild and Frivolous Wants

Many of these areas will overlap, but the categories get you thinking. Later you will collapse these areas into just six or eight.

What you will find once you start to sort and to work with your sticky notes is that there the magic begins to happen. Even greater and better ideas emerge and how all of these fit together begins to fall into place. Please remember to use sticky post-it notes because you will need to move them around, throw some out, create new ones, throw some more out and create even better ones. Put all of your post-it notes in a scrapbook. Yes, go buy a scrapbook rather than a journal or notebook. And, buy a big one while you're at it. Why? Because you will need it later. Go on, do it! Go be a big kid and buy yourself a big scrapbook. You will love this exercise once you get started, and what you do here will affect the rest of your life –it is your way to an abundance of health, wealth, happiness, and love. It could even make you rich and famous. This is not small stuff.

> What you will find once you start to sort and to work with your sticky notes is that magic begins to happen. Even greater and better ideas emerge and how all of these fit together begins to fall into place.

Do a couple of things with this process that are a little wild and ridiculous and even crazy. Also get very small and detailed. Go from the sublime to the ridiculous. Get everything down and out of your brain. Unload and dump your brain of all of your wants and desires. Think of anything and everything that they might possibly be. We are going to be looking for themes and they will emerge more easily the more you have used your imagination. Imagination is the magic and operative word here. Do not worry about the "hows."

People generally accomplish their goals much sooner than the five year plan discussed here, and they frequently say that they should have thought bigger. This is a powerful process.

The *FuturePac* is six to eight five year goals that will emerge from your work with the sticky notes. This *FuturePac* is important because it is an intermediary step in finding your *VisioNavigator* and anchoring your sense of meaning and purpose in life. It and *MasteRevelation* are later chapters in this book. These ideas will be furthered there.

Take your sticky notes with you to work, as you travel, go to the theater, play and have fun, and wherever else you go. Just take a pad of them along and keep jotting what comes to you sometimes in the most unlikely of places. The more you write the more will come and many will merge into a single idea in the end.

Sorting

After you have 10-20 post-it notes written for each area, sort them into the 15 categories specified above. As you do so, you may want to discard what doesn't seem to fit. But, be slow to do this, because any want or desire you wrote down may be something you touched upon that will open many more doors.

First, sort your notes into their correct categories. You will have several pages of each of the categories. ***See if you can collapse your sticky notes into no more that six to eight categories.*** Then, put your sticky notes in order from most significant to least significant. Organize them over a period of a few days. Leave what you have done alone for while and then come back another day and look at your notes and categories once again. You will bring a new and fresh perception each time you work with them.

Once you have your sticky notes in place, it is time to start for-mulating a goal that states where you want to be in five years. Write the goal in the present tense, do not use words like I "will" or any words that put the goals in the future. Keep them in the present tense. Instead of saying, "I want a new house", write, "I have a new house." Instead of writing that you want a new computer, write that you have a new computer. Instead of wanting higher spiritual con-sciousness, write "I have exponentially higher spiritual conscious-ness". Write that you have it and that it is already yours. Write your five year goals in the present tense **as though they have already happened**. Do not use the future tense.

You will find that as you write each of your goals your sense of wholeness in your world will increase and a sense of direction will unfold. This doesn't need to be said with a lot of fanfare and description. It is just so. It just happens when you do the exercise. As unlikely as it sounds, there are profound consequences for doing the exercise.

If you are afraid that it will tie you down too much and limit your thinking, I want to assure you that it will do just the opposite. Remember, the brain moves from generalization to specificity. Everything happens from a point of decision, even if the decision creates more alternatives and even more options. Everything happens from a point of decision. Your life can't move forward until you clarify what you want. It is a start and any goal may be changed. These goals are forever malleable, and many will change in the next five years.

> Everything happens from a point of decision.

Three month action plans

After you have written down each of the five year goals and they are complete, take a break before you go back and edit and rewrite. Then, begin this step. Write down three things that you could go do immediately to move toward your five year goals. They need to be concrete things that you could do in the next three months. They may be very small steps like making a phone call or checking out something on the internet. Each goal should have three-month action plans. These action plans are then connected to your strengths. Write down what strengths you will use to accomplish each one of your identified three-month steps. Tap into your strengths and you will find all of the ability to do what you need to over the next three months. Be sure you identify strengths you have that match the action that you need to take.

Now here is the big difference between the five-year vision goals and the three-month action steps. The five-year goals are malleable while the three-month action plans have to be done. Don't write down something you won't do because once you write it down and commit to it, you have to do it. The reason is that this action will open the door to the next action. If there is no action, no new doors open. Do the next indicated step to ensure that the next steps emerge. You have to be engaged in doing what you can do as a sign that you are opening up to receive what you have said is your five-year goal. This doesn't mean that you have to struggle or push to do any of these action steps. If the action steps are not an emerging flow from having written your goals, then don't put them in the plan. These action steps should be just emerging, having clarified your five-year goals. They are very doable. And doing them will lead you to the next three-month action plans. These are the next obvious steps that you can take. Working in this manner also takes your mind off worrying about whether or not you should be "doing something". You already are. You are doing the most immediate and obvious things that you can do and leaving the rest to the Universe. At the same time, these three-month steps are dynamically getting you ready in ways you can't yet fathom.

Later, in the *MasteRevelation* chapter you will discover the importance of working with vital friends - that will enable your revelation about your future to unfold for you. It will not happen alone. It will happen as a result of your interaction with others who will help you remain committed and consistent to your three-month goals and to your five-year vision. They will give you wonderful ideas.

However, practical, down to earth, very doable three-month action steps are what the Universe will honor and meet, because doing these steps tests your intentions. Doing them means that you mean it and opens the door to more.

Approach each action step with a sense of accomplishment and success. It is how you do these small very "doable" things that open you to be receptive to the greater things that are coming. I can't say this strongly enough. These small things are magic because they will attract to you people, things, events, and happenings that you wouldn't have previously believed could enter into your world. Some will be small and some will be big, but all will help you unfold the overall accomplishment of your goals. It is these small actions, that are doable, that conspire with the Universe in ways that you can't imagine. The key is consistency. Do them!

I can't say this strongly enough. These small things are magic because they will attract to you people, things, events, and happenings that you wouldn't have previously believed could enter into your world. Some will be small and some will be big, but all will help you unfold the overall accomplishment of your goals. It is these small actions, that are doable, that conspire with the Universe in ways that you can't imagine. The key is consistency.

Work Out #5: *Emotional gym* for *FuturePac*

The Hands Prayer is credited to Dr. Masaro Emoto. There is a wonderful story associated with this exercise that you can read in his book, **Love Thyself, The Message from Water III**. The story is too lengthy to include here, but an exercise in the book is powerful and is used here with the addition of The *Emotional Gym* Workout.

There are three simple lines to the prayer:
(Your name), I respect you.
(Your name), I thank-you.
(Your name), I love you.

To each line of the prayer, add an emotion:

(Your name), I respect you (peace).
(Your name), I thank-you (gratitude).
(Your name), I love you (love for yourself).

Place both of your hands flat together in the traditional praying stance, like a child prays, and use this mantra/prayer several times a day, feeling the feeling of gratitude as you say the prayer.

I believe it contains a kind of vibration that travels, so you may want to picture a person or a situation and send your vibration of this prayer to whatever is your intention.

The *Emotional Gym*

The workout, at this point, is to stay consistent with the exercises in the previous chapters. Rather than add a new exercise, be steady and consistent with what you already have learned. Keep doing those exercises.

1. Pulse the five primary emotions. This builds instant access to positive emotion.

2. Use your 5 cues throughout the day. This exercise also builds instant access.

3. Use the music that evokes emotions. This exercise begins to build duration, making an emotion last for a duration of time. In the next chapter we will add the dimension of intensity.

FuturePac Summary

One of the reasons for great angst of indecision is a brain signaling for synchronicity and less use of psychic energy. We are, indeed, living in a time of great indecision. Bombarded by too much negative information, confronted with an overload of choices and a rapidly-changing technology of delivery systems, indecision is a malaise of our times, and the condition is increasing. Indecision causes your brain great unrest.

Write down anything and everything you want on post-it notes –the sticky ones that you can put somewhere and move around. Start writing and writing every single want and desire on its own post-it note.

What you are doing is getting out of your mind and onto paper a thousand ideas, thoughts, wants and desires. It doesn't matter how little or big or petty or unrealistic each one seems. The key is to just get them all down.

What you will find once you start to sort and to work with your sticky notes is that magic begins to happen. Even greater and better ideas emerge and how all of these fit together begins to fall into place.

You will find that as you write each of your goals your sense of wholeness in your world will increase and a sense of direction will unfold. This doesn't need to be said with a lot of fanfare and description. It is just so. It just happens when you do the exercise. As unlikely as it sounds, there are profound consequences for doing the exercise.

Everything happens from a point of decision

Your life can't move until you clarify what you want. It is a start and any goal may be changed. These goals are forever malleable, and many will change in the next five years.

I can't say this strongly enough. These small things are magic because they will attract to you people, things, events, and happenings that you wouldn't have previously believed could enter into your world. Some will be small and some will be big, but all will help you unfold the overall accomplishment of your goals. It is these small actions, that are doable, that conspire with the Universe in ways that you can't imagine. The key is consistency.

VisioNavigator

You will find and define
the Vision and passion for your life.

Decades ago Napolean Hill wrote **Think and Grow Rich**, as a result of his research with those who had been successful. He discovered that the central ingredient shared by those individuals was a definite aim and desire, which he put in capitals and stressed again and again. More recently, Jim Collins in **Good to Great**, proved empirically the same thing – that the most successful companies have a singular aim and the passion to carry it out. Both authors are men who say that without a central aim and passion or desire, the chance of success would be scattered. In this process, we will find the same thing to be true, even though we have gone about getting there somewhat differently and by a process not delineated by either of these men. You are defining a core aim in your life and it will emerge with the passion behind it necessary for its fulfillment.

> You are defining a core aim in your life and it will emerge with the passion behind it necessary for its fulfillment.

You now have at least six five-year goals with a three-month action plan for each goal. How do you feel? I know. You feel like you have sense of direction, that something has come together and sort of locked into place, like a plane, with a designated route to fly. You feel like you know where you're going. And no matter how many times these five-year goals change, and they likely will, they will still provide that basic sense of direction. They are, remember, highly malleable. Form them and shape them as you go along and discover what you learn in the process of moving toward them. Some may change altogether, but they will be replaced by others. When one door closes, or when you close the door, another door opens and you will know what and where that door is.

In doing your *FuturePac*, you have experienced a sense of relief, a release of some of the energy of resistance that comes from not knowing or not being sure of where you want to go. You have released the energy of indecision and resistance; now with that extra released energy, you move your journey up a notch, and that is to vision. In much the same way that you used the sticky post-it notes to come up with six or more five-year goals, you now begin to use the six goals in the same way to realize your vision.

Your vision in life is what you want to accomplish with your life; it is how you use your life. And you can't go wrong. Just being here in this life and wanting what you want is enough. The energy of the wanting and the desires pushes the bounds of the Universe; it adds to the energy of the Universe, so you have already succeeded just by being here and having wants and desires.

The energy and vibrations of our six goals is an energy that adds to the energy in the Universe and pushes its boundaries. This is what you are here for, to add to this energy that pushes the edges of the Universe further, by the nature of the energy of your wanting. You're already successful, just by your being.

However, it is more fun than that. We can have what we want. A vision is a significant and important part, because it culminates, through attraction, in the fulfillment of your six goals. It is like a giant magnet that attracts the general, rather than the specific. Your vision brings all of what is behind the goals. It is this vision that attracts your overall good – peace, serenity, contentment, fulfillment, joy, happiness, goodness- all that is good in a general sense.

> A vision is a significant and important part, because it culminates, through attraction, in the fulfillment of your six goals. It is like a giant magnet that attracts the general, rather than the specific. Your vision brings all of what is behind the goals.

Your vision emerges from immersing yourself in your six goals. As you consider them, write about them, meditate upon them; a vision of what gives your life meaning will begin to emerge. It will emerge as your passion. Your vision is about how you will add your nature, or your soul, to the Universe and give it your "stamp". Your vision is your passion and your legacy. It is what you want to accomplish with your life. And it comes, over a period of time, by allowing these six or more goals to work, forming a larger picture that defines what it is that you are after in your life in a full, whole way. Your vision is "you" - which you uniquely and idiosyncratically give back to the world.

My vision is to teach as many people as possible how to stay in the *UpSpiral* and to find their vision for their own life. That's it. It's just that simple, but powerful in its implications.

It is the expression of how you define your significance in the world. What are you here for? How do you want to give that back to the Universe?

I want to draw a distinction here between a "life purpose" or purpose-driven life and a vision. I don't want your life to be driven by anything and I am suspect of the word "purpose" because it is too specific, too narrow and too limited. But it does describe a part of this picture. Your vision can be your purpose and it can be specific and that's fine; it is part of the picture. In a sense, my own vision is a purpose and it passes the test of giving me a sense of significance. That is the acid test of a vision. Does it give you a sense of significance? And more than driven - is it inspired?

I want to draw a distinction here between a "life purpose" or purpose-driven life and a vision. I don't want your life to be driven by anything and I am suspect of the word "purpose" because it is too specific, too narrow and too limited.

A vision doesn't necessarily mean that you are to accomplish a certain thing or that you are accomplishing anything. Your vision can be to live a life of love and to love everyone you meet. Will Rogers said, "I never met a man I didn't like". That could be a vision with great significance. Consider the good healthy vibrations that you would be sending into the world. A vision could be painting the most beautiful paintings you are able to produce. A vision is the expression of you that you want to uniquely express to the world in your own way. Your vision may be to live as a person of peace in every circumstance and to let the ripples of that peace move out through the pond of humanity.

That is the acid test of a vision. Does it give you a sense of significance? And more than driven- is it inspired?

A purpose expresses doing a "something". A vision expresses you giving back to the Universe, in the way or with the medium, that best expresses you and energy released through you. The test is this: Does it give you a sense of significance? Does your vision give you a sense of being and place in the universe that is meaningful? It is this sense, that who you are is significant and meaningful in the total picture, that is important. Doing something may be one of the expressions of that. You may not have an airtight purpose to accomplish something absolutely specific. The work is you; the vision is expressing the fullness of you in your own unique way. You don't have to produce or accomplish a single visible or tangible thing.

> Does your vision give you a sense of being and place in the universe that is meaningful? It is this sense, that who you are is significant and meaningful in the total picture, that is important. Doing something may be one of the expressions of that. You may not have an airtight purpose to accomplish something absolutely specific.

Suppose your vision is making your yard a place of peace and beauty for those who pass by. Is that sufficient enough to qualify as a vision? The acid test: Does it give you a sense of significance and personal meaning? Is the energy of the Universe expressing through you?

Everybody has something different to give back, to offer and to share, that is an expression of their self-fulfillment and desire to give back to others and to the Universe. Its size and scope, tangible or not, doesn't matter. What matters is whether or not it gives you a sense of significance and meaning.

A vision could be to stay in a place of peace and flow - as an example to the world - of how this flow gives you a sense of your own personal significance and meaning. My grandmother, in her 70's, thought of herself as very insignificant. But, in reality, her being, her love, her approval, and what she could see in others made her, right to her death, an anchor for the growth of others around her. She helped others define who they were and often ignited their self-confidence. While she did not see her significance, she leaves a legacy of people who would say that they are as they are, in many ways, due to her influence in their lives. I know. I was one of them.

A Sense of Personal Significance

What is this? A sense of personal significance is tied to what I call your meaning making system or your meaning making scheme – it is how you make meaning out of the world. Without this sense of "meaning-making", people flatline, go into the *DownSpiral* and become depressed. That is what happens much of the time. A lot of the time, it doesn't go all the way to depression, but stops instead with the flatline. People flatline in life when they have no sense of personal significance or meaning making. This is when they start having affairs, shop too much, or buy things they don't need or even really want.

> A sense of personal significance is tied to what I call your meaning making system or your meaning making scheme – it is how you make meaning out of the world. Without this sense of "meaning-making", people flatline, go into the *DownSpiral* and become depressed.

Sometime ago, I had a client who brought in a shoe box full of medications, prescribed by her physician, psychiatrist, and a longevity institute. She had flatlined and nothing would help. As soon as I convinced her that she was responsible for her own *UpSpiral*, she became *StrengthSmart* and started to want and to desire again. Today, she would tell you that she wanted to die because the meaning had gone out of her life. People find all kinds of ways - many of them addictive - to distract themselves from the experience that they are emotionally and intellectually flatlining. While it seems they are neither up nor down, they are actually down because their life experience is pretty empty. It may not be an emptiness that is felt, but experienced in eating too much, watching too much television, moving too much, changing jobs too often, not being able to remain in relationships, changing friends, or changing clothes three times a day. It can be seen in running to the next movie or the next popular fad, anything that fills that sense of a lack of meaning and significance. You can only stick an IPOD in your ears and a one-inch screen in front of your face for so long, before flatlining has to be expressed in another way. You may start drinking too much coffee or riding your motorcycle too fast. Perhaps your temperament is snappy and short, and you have little patience with others because, in reality, you have little patience with yourself. Flat is flat - and usually irritable.

Perhaps you collect dolls. You don't just collect them, but crave them. In fact, you have three times as many of them as you really want with no place to put them. Now this is not necessarily flatlining; it may be that you just appreciate dolls. Do the dolls really provide a sense of significance and meaning? Or are they a response to flatlining because you do not have a clear vision or sense of significance in life? You have to be the judge of whether or not the things with which you fill your life are expressions of your vision. What if all these dolls give you pleasure and you enjoy them? Enjoyment and pleasure are far from flatlining. If you know you enjoy them and they give you pleasure, then your pleasure is added to the goodness of the world. But only you know if they give you pleasure or if they don't.

Here is a good test. Are they the outcomes of your six, five-year goals? Are they a measure of moving in your life to where you really want to be? Do they fit your vision?

The VisioNavigator is, in part, your six five-year goals. They are, if you have been thorough and complete in doing them, navigating you to a sense of your vision in life.

The VisioNavigator is, in part, your six five-year goals. They are, if you have been thorough and complete in doing them, navigating you to a sense of your vision in life.

Your inner *VibeCore* is also a part of this navigation. Remember that this core is a measure of knowing what you want and believing that you will get it. The *VibeCore* is like a flywheel pushing you toward the realization of your own vision. Your strengths are also working to move you in this direction. But most of the cumulative effect of your six five- year goals is silently, or not so silently, navigating you toward a sense of this vision.

But most of the cumulative affect of your six five-year goals are silently, or not so silently, navigating you toward a sense of this vision.

This vision is a sense of what you can be the best at doing, your own personal best at doing, and it is what you are passionate about. This vision grabs you in such a way that you want to do it, you can't help but do it, because it's just an extension of you, it's just you in the world. Your *FuturePac* just leads you to your vision and then the vision navigates you onward to more of its own personal expression. The vision will navigate the vision and you will be amazed where it will take you, the doors you will open, and the people you will meet. You won't believe the people that you will meet nor will you believe how you meet them. Situations will occur that you could never have planned. They pop out of nowhere and they happen so easily that you want, at first, not to trust them, but they are so uncanny that you know that you must. If you keep working the three-month steps of your *FuturePac,* the flywheel that keeps turning will lead you to your vision and your vision will lead you to the people who will help you bring it about.

This vision will take you so far, in fact, that it will bring you to the people who can most help you achieve it. This is where we go next, to the *MasteRevelation*

Your *VisioNavigator* is the cumulative energy from your *FuturePac,* from your six, five-year goals, and as you form your vision and write it down, the force of the vision will navigate you further on. This is not difficult; it is not pushing and shoving or hard work. It just happens; it comes and you move forward in your thinking. If you are pushing and trying too hard, it will elude you.

Your *VisioNavigator* is the cumulative energy from your *FuturePac,* from your six, five-year goals, and as you form your vision and write it down, the force of the vision will navigate you further on.

Here is the process to the *VisioNavigator:*

1. You have six, five-year goals and three-month action steps for each one. Look at these from a holistic point of view. What is the overall theme? What does all of this say to you? Where does it lead you? What comes up intuitively for you? What is very apparent and just jumps out in your face?

2. What would you like to do, that is your vision, for what you want to be an expression of the significance and meaning of your life? Write it down. Don't labor at it. Just write it down as it comes, maybe all at once, or maybe over time, but write it down. Write

down what comes. Don't edit it and don't censor it or second guess it. Just write it down. It's not cast in stone; you can change it.

3. Let your goals lead you into your vision and your vision will navigate you from there. Your five year goals and your three-month plan is a flywheel of progress; it unfolds as you put it into motion. Goals are designed for you to reach in a certain direction. They give direction and forward moving momentum to your unfolding consciousness. *Goals, in and of themselves, may not, in the end, be as significantly important as what they point toward or where they take you next. Goals are doorways to vision and that vision sometimes takes some time to unfold and navigate itself where it wants to go. But it will unfold. Underneath this vision lies your passion.*

In the book **Good to Great**, this vision is called your "hedgehog concept". Businesses that are great define what is called their "hedgehog" concept first, and their goals grow out of that vision. This is the empirical research that proves the importance of vision at the level of great companies. It is this that distinguishes companies that are great, rather than merely good. The hedgehog concept is what you do best, what you are passionate about. That may well have been expressed in your goals. It may already be in your goal statement. However, I have found that many people don't start with this concept clear in their minds and have to find it. As the use of strengths unfold and as your *VibeCore* increases, as deep calls unto what is deeper, if it hasn't already, your vision will emerge.

> *Goals, in and of themselves, may not, in the end, be as significantly important as what they point toward or where they take you next. Goals are doorways to vision and that vision sometimes takes some time to unfold and navigate itself where it wants to go. But it will unfold. Underneath this vision lies your passion.*

Jim Collins not only wrote **Good to Great** but also wrote **Built to Last**. Although he wrote **Built to Last** first, he sees the second book, **Good to Great** actually as the prequel to **Built to Last**. **Built to Last** is about identifying core values and identifying your strengths. By reading this book you have already begun to get at your core values. In letting these strengths unfold in a *FuturePac*, you have put these values in a kind of action plan that is value-laden with what is important to you. As you allow yourself to value what you value, and go after what you value, your vision will navigate you. It will bring its revelations. And with that word revelation we move onto to the next chapter, *MasteRevelation*. If you're following the process, that's where you're headed.

Workout #6: *Emotional Gym* for *VisioNavigator*

Each of your six goals is assigned an emotion that belongs to it. Certitude and assurance are now added to the five primary emotions of gratitude, love, peace, joy, and hope.

Every time you look at your goals, think about them, or meditate about them, attach the emotion or feeling to the goal. As you go through your day, think of your goals and the smaller steps you are taking to attain them, and feel the feeling attached to them. Feel the feeling in the now.

Every day, read your goals at least once and feel the feeling that you have attached to each of the goals. Napoleon Hill told his students to read their goals once in the morning and once in the evening. Jim Collins, in **Good to Great**, gives assurance that the hedgehog concept never got out of the sight of the great leaders. Keep your goals palpably close to you, but not in an insistent or demanding way. Just wear them loosely and don't be afraid to change the goal. Emotions tell the subjective mind that what you have set as goals is important and that keeps them in both the conscious and unconscious mind.

The significance of this exercise is that you are exercising the particular abilities of the left hemisphere to move emotions and the content to which the emotions are attached, into subjective or unconscious memory. The evidence for this is based on information that is called "split brain" research. It is enough for our purposes here to note that attaching feeling to goals sink them more quickly and deeply into the unconscious mind.

So, each day, read your goals or, even better, write them down in a journal, and as you speak them or write them, add an emotional feeling to them that is part of your *Emotional Gym.*

Read your goals, with emotions behind them, everyday.

Add your sensory system to your experience.

Sandpaper

One way to sink your goals into your sensory system is to write them with your fingers on sandpaper. Lightly spell out the goal on sandpaper, and your system of touch gets more invested in your goal and invests the part of your brain that communicates by touch, to "touch" the rest of your brain. When your goals seem to slip away or they seem to be faintly removed from you, as they do from time to time, as though they are unreachable or just a dream, take out the sandpaper and wake up your sensory system. See what happens to your dreams and goals; they start to come alive, in a short time.

Smell

The olfactory system is one of the most powerful systems in the brain and certainly one of the oldest. A smell can transport us to another whole world of memories, a smell can take you instantly to another reality.

I once picked up an old piece of screen wire, the kind that used to be made of metal, and the smell instantly transported me to being 4 years old with my nose up against my grandmother's front screen door. I was back on her front porch again, transported powerfully by just a smell.

Assign each of your goals a smell. Smell the odor, or even think of the odor and assign it to one of your goals. You will be surprised how often you then begin to encounter this odor when you least expect it. Practice associating smell and the olfactory system with your goal, and it will help to take your whole consciousness of intentionality to another level.

Intensity

Intensity is the last measure of emotional muscle. You have learned immediacy and duration of positive emotions. Now increase the intensity level of a "3" or a "4" of an emotion to a level of "7" or more. "Raise the volume" of your experience of positive emotions by increasing the intensity.

VisioNavigator Summary

You are defining a core aim in your life and it will emerge with the passion behind it necessary for its fulfillment.

A vision is a significant and important part, because it culminates, through attraction, in the fulfillment of your six goals. It is like a giant magnet that attracts the general, rather than the specific. Your vision brings all of what is behind the goals.

I want to draw a distinction here between a "life purpose" or purpose-driven life and a vision. I don't want your life to be driven by anything and I am suspect of the word "purpose" because it is too specific, too narrow and too limited.

That is the acid test of a vision. Does it give you a sense of significance? And more than driven- is it inspired?

Does your vision give you a sense of being and place in the universe that is meaningful? It is this sense, that who you are is significant and meaningful in the total picture, that is important. Doing something may be one of the expressions of that. You may not have an airtight purpose to accomplish something absolutely specific.

A sense of personal significance is tied to what I call your meaning making system or your meaning making scheme – it is how you make meaning out of the world. Without this sense of "meaning-making", people flatline, go into the *DownSpiral* and become depressed.

The VisioNavigator is, in part, your six five-year goals. They are, if you have been thorough and complete in doing them, navigating you to a sense of your vision in life.

But most of the cumulative effect of your six five-year goals is silently, or not so silently, navigating you toward a sense of this vision.

Your *VisioNavigator* is the cumulative energy from your *FuturePac*, from your six, five-year goals, and as you form your vision and write it down, the force of the vision will navigate you further on.

Goals, in and of themselves, may not in the end, be significantly important as to what they point toward or to where they take you next. Goals are doorways to vision and that vision sometimes takes some time to unfold and navigate itself where it wants to go. But it will unfold. Underneath this vision lies your passion.

MasteRevelation

Revelation emerges from the synchronicity of the minds of vital friends.

You have been following a design that emerges naturally and gradually. The *UpSpiral* is sustained and your ability to remain in it is enabled by finding out your strengths and becoming *StrengthSmart*. You have learned to build positive emotional muscle that always moves you toward the positive; it has become the direction of the "lean" or the disposition in your mind. It is the "élan" of your mood. As you have learned to use your strengths automatically and reflexively, you are increasingly aware of your wants and your desires. Your *VibeCore* strengthens and builds; you are better able to know what you want and you believe that you are going to get it. As it strengthens, deeper wants and desires bubble up and emerge in you. They come from the creative depths where your strengths come from. They come from the real you. Your *FuturePac* is the organization of those wants and desires into a kind of overall, very flexible, malleable plan that life will change and alter, but to which life will also deliver your desires.

As the *FuturePac* becomes firm, your vision emerges and it navigates you onward. And as the flywheel of your *VisioNavigator* works for you an amazing thing begins to happen.

You begin to attract into your life the people you need along the way through your journey. Some of these people will be old friends that you see and know in new ways. Some old friends will move away and drop pretty much out of the picture of your life. But most amazing of all, some new magic friends will show up. Well, it will seem like magic.

> You begin to attract into your life, the people you need along the way through your journey.

Tom Rath, author of the book **Vital Friends**, identifies the significant people in our lives, not only by a test you can take, but also by research and insight into exactly who are vital friends for us and exactly what functions (they are specific) they serve in our lives. What Tom Rath rediscovers in **Vital Friends** is close to the concept of the Master Mind, re-invigorated in our day. Rath recognizes how wholly significant vital friends are to our lives. The book includes an ID code to give you access to Rath's **Vital Friends** Assessment and website. The test sheds light on the roles your friends play in your life. It is from this Master Mind of vital friends that *MasteRevelation* springs alive.

What I am going to encourage you to do is to experience the revelation that occurs from paying attention to the friends your *VisioNavigator* will bring to you. Some you have, some you don't have yet. Take these people into a new kind of Master Mind group.

Napoleon Hill is the father of the Master Mind concept. He realized that where "two or three are gathered together" there is something that happens. The important distinguishing factor that Hill speaks of is, this group must also have a partner called "harmony" that brings and holds this group together.

A Master Mind group is simply this. It is a group of people who help you to achieve the goals in your FuturPac, who remind you of your vision and your core values, and who, by their suggestions, bring revelation into your life. It is almost magical! The Master Mind will lift you to a new level of consciousness and awareness beyond the limits of your own vision. Answers that you would never have gotten come through your Master Mind group. There is a level of awareness that the Master Mind group achieves that is really revelation. Not only do doors open and connections happen, but the awareness it creates moves the flywheel of your vision forward much more rapidly. This all occurs when you bring together your vital friends and you talk with them on a regular basis.

A Master Mind group works best when everyone is helping everyone else achieve their goals and their vision. But a Master Mind group can start with you asking at least one person to help you stick to your vision and to give you advice and suggestions on how to get there. At least that's where it starts.

First, you are going to be amazed at the people who come into your life, and who are willing to help you and guide you. Even though you still have to listen to your own inner voice, their help will bring revelation to you.

> There is a level of awareness that the Master Mind group achieves that is really revelation. Not only do doors open and connections happen, but the awareness it creates moves the flywheel of your vision forward much more rapidly. This all occurs when you bring together your vital friends and you talk with them on a regular basis.

Your Master Mind group may only have one other person. It may only start or continue with one other person you talk and work with every week. Make the other person a vital friend and identify them by using Tom Rath's book; it's a wonderful guide for finding and knowing who you should consider for your group member/s.

None of us is the "Lone Ranger." Certainly when it comes to a vision, we need the revelation that comes from others.

But what really is "revelation?" Revelation means that others will cause you to look at things you do not see, recognize opportunities that you cannot find and point you in directions you would otherwise not have gone on your own. It is the missing factor in many people's journey, although it is, in one way or another, a part of every successful person's journey.

Revelation is a revealing of an inspired truth. As an inspired truth, revelation causes you to see and approach things, oftentimes surprisingly and radically different than you might otherwise do. Keep in mind, though, that a subtle shift in your consciousness caused by a remark or nudge from a Master Mind partner can change your whole approach.

Revelation is what wakes us up when we are interacting with other people. Revelation happens when we open our lives to others and let them in on our plans and let them fertilize our thinking. Revelation enhances your *VibeCore* and it comes from relating to other people. **The revelation that comes from this interaction with vital friends, with sharing your goals and vision and being held accountable by others, increases the strength of clearly identifying what you want, remaining consistent with your core values or goals and it increases your belief that you can have what you want.**

But what really is "revelation"? Revelation means that others will cause you to look at things you do not see, recognize opportunities that you cannot find and point you in directions you would otherwise not have gone on your own.

A lot of the time, we think that revelation comes from some big supernatural experience. Revelation happens through our interaction with other people. The "Aha" is a result, most often, of some kind of interaction with others. It is just the nature of the Universe that revelation happens in the union of harmony and sharing with others who are our vital friends.

For some reason, it is just intended that we take each other along. We need it and are nourished by it; our dreams are nurtured and supported the strongest when our Master Mind group makes revelation happen. It's called *MasteRevelation*, and you need it in your life.

This cross-fertilization of a shared unity of knowledge and desire not only helps you but it helps everyone concerned grow as well. It is the way things were meant to develop. Every great person has had access to *MasteRevelation* through either an "accidentally" created group of vital friends or through one that was created with these needs and ideas in mind.

For some reason, it is just intended that we take each other along. We need it and are nourished by it; our dreams are nurtured and supported the strongest when our Master Mind group makes revelation happen. It's called *MasteRevelation*, and you need it in your life.

Your vibration depends upon your vital friends and your use of them. Everybody who has sustained the forward motion of their own personal flywheel has them. And you know it is true; these vital friends and their believing in us have kept the "mojo" of our flywheel moving. It is the "salt of our earth".

The really big jumps, the really big satisfaction and the really marked advances in your consciousness will occur from *MasteRevelation* groups and associations.

Jim Collins, in **Good to Great** talks about the "flywheel" of a business, as the activity that you keep pushing and moving over a period of time causing it to grow and gather momentum. It is the flywheel of ongoing necessary activity, which happens over a period of time, that just keeps going and starts long before great results are seen. That flywheel has got to turn in your life and it will turn faster and better when you develop relationships with vital friends who keep it turning with you. It turns and gathers its momentum from one solitary piece of the formula that is absolutely essential: the people who comprise your *MasteRevelation* group must believe in and support your vision. They believe you and believe in you. What we need most are the people who believe in us at the times when our own "mojo" is low. Every successful person has vital friends and no one has ever gone it alone and succeeded. Everybody has got somebody who kept their "mojo" working when they either could not, or were at a very low place in their *VibeCore*.

Your vibration is enhanced by your vital friends and your use of them. Everybody who has sustained the forward motion of their own personal flywheel has them. And you know it is true; these vital friends and their believing in us have kept the "mojo" of our flywheel moving. It is the "salt of our earth".

Recognize the vital friends you already have and consider attracting one or two more. Start by plugging into your vital friend/s on a regular basis and let them help you plan the steps of your ongoing vision and hold you to a degree of accountability. Revelation will be the result.

Workout #7: *Emotional Gym* **for** *MasteRevelation*

1. Continue to work with the Emotional Gym exercises. You have learned to have instant access to your emotions. You have learned how to increase the duration of these emotions and you have learned how to increase the intensity of them. Now go back to the first exercise of feeling the five feelings, gratitude, love, peace, joy, and hope 10 times a day at a level of a 4 or 5. Build this exercise throughout your day and "pulse" the emotions. That is, you will feel a little of them over and over again at just a low level. The constant low level of positive emotion is more significant than several intense periods of positive emotion and they affect over all mood more.

2. The *Emotional Gym*

With this exercise we begin to work on the last dimension of building emotional muscle. Use the music you have assigned to the five emotions. You now have a piece of music that elicits each of the five primary emotions. You have practiced, with this music, making the emotion last (duration) throughout the music. Now, as you feel the emotion with each piece of music, allow the intensity to build to a 6 or 7, experience that you can increase the intensity of the emotions. It is not necessary to feel ecstatic or blissful. Remember, our goal is to "feel good", so raise the intensity of each emotion to a 6 or 7 on our scale of 1-10. 1 is a little emotion, 10 is an enormous amount of the emotion. This is the measure of "intensity" in building emotional muscle.

3. Get a copy of **Vital Friends** by Tom Rath, read it and take the test that is there.

4. One final caveat. After this influence and cross-fertilization of ideas with **vital friends,** you must in the end follow your own inner knowing.

MasteRevelation **Summary**

You begin to attract into your life, the people you need along the way through your journey.

What I am going to encourage you to do is to experience the revelation that occurs from paying attention to the friends your *VisioNavigator* will bring to you. Some you have, some you don't have yet. Take these people into a new kind of Master Mind group.

There is a level of awareness that the Master Mind group achieves that is really revelation. Not only do doors open and connections happen, but the awareness it creates moves the flywheel of your vision forward much more rapidly. This all occurs when you bring together your vital friends and you talk with them on a regular basis.

But what really is "revelation"? Revelation means that others will cause you to look at things you do not see, recognize opportunities that you cannot find and point you in directions you would otherwise not have gone on your own.

The revelation that comes from this interaction with others, with sharing your goals and vision and being held accountable by others, increases the strength of clearly identifying what you want, remaining consistent with your core values or goals and it increases your belief that you can have what you want.

For some reason, it is just intended that we take each other along. We need it and are nourished by it; our dreams are nurtured and supported the strongest when our Master Mind group makes revelation happen. It's called *MasteRevelation*, and you need it in your life.

Your vibration depends upon your vital friends and your use of them. Everybody who has sustained the forward motion of their own personal flywheel has them. And you know it is true; these vital friends and their believing in us have kept the "mojo" of our flywheel moving. It is the "salt of our earth".

One final caveat. After this influence and cross-fertilization of ideas with **vital friends,** you must in the end follow your own inner knowing.

References

PROMISE 1

American Psychiatratic Association, **DSM IV, The Diagnostic and Statistical Manual of Mental Disorders**, 2005, Fourth Edition, American Psychiatric Association, Washington, D.C.

Pert, Candace, **The Molecules of Emotion: The Science Behind Mind Body Medicine**, 2005 New York, Scribner

Goldberg, Elkhonon, **The Executive Brain: Frontal Lobes and The Civilized Mind**, 2001, Oxford Press, New York

Csikszentmihalyi, Mihalyi, **Good Business**, 2003, Viking, New York

Lipton, Bruce, **The Biology of Belief**, 2005, Elite Books, Santa Rosa

Gilbert, Dan, **Stumbling on Happiness**, 2006, Alfred A. Knopf, New York

PROMISE 2

Collins, Jim, **Good To Great**, 2001, Harper Collins, New York

Seligman, Martin, E. P., and Peterson, Christopher **Learned Helplessness: A Theory for the Age of Personal Control**, 1995 New York: Oxford University Press.

Fredrickson, Barbara, **Handbook of Positive Psychology**, 2005, Oxford University Press

Fredrickson, Barbara, *The role of positive emotions in positive psychology: The broaden-and-build theory of positive emotions.* **American Psychologist** 56: 218-226

Goldberg, Eklhonon, **The Wisdom Paradox; How Your Mind Can Grow Stronger As Your Brain Grows Older**, 2005, Gotham Books, The Penguin Group, New York

Mueller, Robert, **Most of All They Taught Me Happiness**, 1978, Doubleday and Co., New York

Katie, Byron, **Loving What Is**, 2002, Crown Rivers Press, New York

PROMISE 3

Schwartz, Barry and Begley, Sharon, **The Mind and The Brain, Neuroplasticity and the Power of Mental Force**, 2002, Harper Collins, New York

Peterson, Chris, and Seligman, Martin E. P, **Character Strengths and Virtues**, 2004, Oxford University Press, New York

Buckingham, Marcus, and Clifton, Donald, **Now, Discover Your Strengths**, 2001, Simon and Schuster, New York

Dick, Gris, **The New Soviet Psychic Discoveries**, 1978, Prentice Hall, Englewood Cliffs, New Jersey

Seligman, Martin, **Authentic Happiness**, 2002, Simon and Schuster, New York

Rath, Tom, **Strengthsfinder 2.0**, 2007, Gallup Press, New York

Hicks, Esther and Jerry, **Ask And It Is Given**, 2004, Hayhouse, Carlsbad, CA

PROMISE 4

Csikszentmihaly, Mihaly, **Flow: The Psychology of Optimal Behavior**, 1990, Harper and Row, New York

Seligman, Dr. Martin, **Learned Optimism**, 1990, Simon and Schuster, New York

PROMISE 5

Emoto, Masaro, **Love Thyself, The Message from Water III**, 2004, Hay House, Inc., Carlsbad, CA

PROMISE 6

Hill, Napoleon, **Think and Grow Rich**, Ross Cornwell, ed., Aventine Press, San Diego

Collins, Jim, **Good To Great**, 2001, Harper Collins, New York

Collins, Jim, **Built to Last**, 2002, Harper Collins, New York

Scott, Trevor, www.BeverlyHillsHypnosis.com, Beverly Hills

LeDoux, Joseph, **The Emotional Brain**, 1996, Touchstone, New York

PROMISE 7

Rath, Tom, **Vital Friends**, 2006, Gallup Press, New York

Hill, Napoleon, **Law of Success**, 2003, Highland Hill Media Group, Los Angeles

Bibliography

PROMISE 1

American Psychiatratic Association. **DSM V, The Diagnostic and Statistical Manual of Mental Disorders**, 2013, Fifth edition, American Psychiatric Association, Washington, D.C.

Pert, Candace. **The Molecules of Emotion: The Science Behind Mind Body Medicine**, 2005, Scribner, New York

Goldberg, Elkhonon. **The Executive Brain: Frontal Lobes and The Civilized Mind**, 2001, Oxford Press, New York

Csikszentmihalyi, Mihalyi. **Good Business**, 2003, Viking, New York

Lipton, Bruce. **The Biology of Belief**, 2005, Elite Books, Santa Rosa

Gilbert, Dan. **Stumbling on Happiness**, 2006, Alfred A. Knopf, New York

Schwartz, Jeffrey. **Brain Lock**, 1998, Harper Collins, New York

Seung, Sebastian. **Connectome: How The Brain's Wiring Makes Us Who We Are**, 2012, Houghton Mifflin Harcourt, Boston

Fredrickson, Barbara. **Positivity**, 2009, Crown, New York

Merzenich, Michael M. **Soft-Wired: How the New Science of Brain Plasticity Can Change Your Life**, 2013, Parnassus

Holt-Lunstad, J., Smith, T. B., & Layton, J. B. (2010). *Social relationships and mortality risk: A meta-analytic review.* **PLoS Medicine**, 7(7):e1000316. doi:10.1371/journal.pmed.1000316

Danner, D. D., Snowdon, D. A., & Friesen, W. V. (2001). *Positive emotions in early life and longevity: Findings from the Nun study.* **Journal of Personality and Social Psychology**, 80(5), 804–813.

PROMISE 2

Collins, Jim. **Good To Great**, 2001, Harper Collins, New York

Davidson, Richard J and Begley, Sharon. **The Emotional Life Of Your Brain: How Its Unique Patterns Affect The Way You Think, Feel, and Live-and How You Can Change Them**, 2012, Hudson Street Press, New York

Frances, Allen. **Saving Normal: An Insider's Revolt Against Out-of-Control Psychiatric Diagnosis, DSM-5, Big Pharma, and the Medicalization of Ordinary Life**, 2013, William Morrow, New York

Seligman, Martin E. P., and Peterson, Christopher. **Learned Helplessness: A Theory for the Age of Personal Control**, 1995, Oxford University Press, New York

Fredrickson, Barbara. **Handbook of Positive Psychology**, 2005, Oxford University Press

Fredrickson, Barbara. *The role of positive emotions in positive psychology: The broaden-and-build theory of positive emotions.* **American Psychologist** 56: 218-226

Fredrickson, Barbara. **Love 2.0: How Our Supreme Emotion Affects Everything We Think, Do, Feel, and Become**, 2013, Hudson Street, New York

Goldberg, Eklhonon. **The Wisdom Paradox; How Your Mind Can Grow Stronger As Your Brain Grows Older**, 2005, Gotham Books, The Penguin Group, New York

Mueller, Robert. **Most of All They Taught Me Happiness**, 1978, Doubleday, New York

Katie, Byron. **Loving What Is, 2002**, Crown Rivers Press, New York

Whitaker, Robert. **Anatomy of an Epidemic: Magic Bullets, Psychiatric Drugs, and the Astonishing Rise of Mental Illness in America**, 2010, Crown, New York

Boehm, J. K., & Kubzansky, L. D. (2012). *The heart's content: The association between positive psychological well-being and cardiovascular health.* **Psychological Bulletin**, 138(4), 655–691.

PROMISE 3

Schwartz, Barry and Begley, Sharon. **The Mind and The Brain, Neuroplasticity and the Power of Mental Force**, 2002, Harper Collins, New York

Doidge, Norman M.D. **The Brain That Changes Itself: Stories Of Personal Triumph from the Frontiers of Brain Science**, 2007, Viking, New York

Peterson, Chris, and Seligman, Martin E. P. **Character Strengths and Virtues**, 2004, oxford University Press, New York

Buckingham, Marcus and Clifton, Donald. **Now, Discover Your Strengths**, 2001, Simon and Schuster, New York

Dick, Gris, **The New Soviet Psychic Discoveries**, 1978, Prentice Hall, Englewood Cliffs, New Jersey

Seligman, Martin E. P. **Authentic Happiness**, 2002, Simon and Schuster, New York

Rath, Tom, **Strengthsfinder** 2.0, 2007, Gallup Press, New York

Hicks, Esther and Jerry. **Ask And It Is Given**, 2004, Hayhouse, Carlsbad, CA

McDermott, Diane and Snyder, **C. R. Making Hope Happen: A Workbook for Turning Possibilities into Reality**, 1999, New Harbinger Publications, Oakland, CA

Linley, Alex. **Average to A+: Realising Strengths in Yourself and Others**, 2008, CAPP, Coventry, U. K.

Peterson, Christopher. **A Primer in Positive Psychology**, 2006, Oxford University Press

Lyubomirsky, Sonja. **The How of Happiness: A New Approach to Getting the Life You Want**, 2008, Penguin, New York

Peterson, Christopher. **Pursuing the Good Life: 100 Reflections on Positive Psychology**, 2013, Oxford University Press

Diener, Ed and Robert Biswas-Diener. **Happiness: Unlocking the Mysteries of Psychological Wealth**, 2008, Blackwell Publishing, Malden, MA

Snyder, C. R., and Shane J. Lopez. **Oxford Handbook of Positive Psychology**, 2009, Oxford University Press

PROMISE 4

Csikszentmihaly, Mihaly. **Flow: The Psychology of Optimal Behavior**, 1990, Harper and Row, New York

Cskiszentmihaly, Mihaly. **Finding Flow: The Psychology of Engagement with Everyday Life**, 1997, Basic Books, New York

Seligman, Martin E. P. **Learned Optimism**, 1990, Simon and Schuster, New York

Seligman, Martin E. P. **Flourish**, 2011, Random House Australia, North Sydney

Porges, Stephen W. **The Polyvagal Theory: Neurophysiological Foundations of Emotions, Attachment, Communication, and Self-regulation**, 2011, W. W. Norton, New York

PROMISE 5

Emoto, Masaro. **Love Thyself, The Message from Water III**, 2004, Hay House, Carlsbad, CA

Seeman, T. E., Lusignolo, T. M., Albert, M., & Berkman, L. (2001). *Social relationships, social support, and patterns of cognitive aging in healthy, high- functioning older adults: MacArthur studies of successful aging.* **Health Psychology**, 20(4), 243–255

Kok, B. E., Coffey, K. A., Cohn, M. A., Catalino, L. I., Vacharkulksemsuk, T., Algoe, S. B., Brantley, M., & Fredrickson, B. L. **Positive emotions drive an upward spiral that links social connections and health.** Psychological Science

Klauser, Henriette Anne. **Write It Down, Make It Happen: Knowing What You Want-- and Getting It!** 2000, Scribner, New York

Goleman, Daniel. **Focus: The Hidden Driver of Excellence**, 2013, Harper, New York

Kahneman, Daniel. **Thinking, Fast and Slow**, 2011, Farrar, Straus and Giroux, New York

Sutton, Robert I., and Hayagreeva Rao. **Scaling up Excellence: Getting to More Without Settling for Less**, 2014, Crown Business

Gladwell, Malcolm. **Outliers: The Story of Success**, 2011, Back Bay Books

Gladwell, Malcolm. **The Tipping Point: How Little Things Can Make a Big Difference**, 2005, Abacus, London

PROMISE 6

Hill, Napoleon. **Think and Grow Rich**, Ross Cornwell, ed., Aventine Press, San Diego

Collins, Jim. **Good To Great**, 2001, Harper Collins, New York

Collins, Jim. **Built to Last**, 2002, Harper Collins, New York

Frankl, Victor. **Man's Search For Meaning**, 1992, Beacon Books, Bosyon

LeDoux, Joseph. **The Emotional Brain**, 1996, Touchstone, New York

Dweck, Carol S. **Mindset**, 2012, Robinson, London

Pink, Daniel H. Drive: **The Surprising Truth about What Motivates Us**, 2009, Riverhead, New York

Duhigg, Charles. **The Power of Habit: Why We Do What We Do in Life and Business**, 2012, Random House, New York

PROMISE 7

Rath, Tom. **Vital Friends**, 2006, Gallup Press, New York

Hill, Napoleon. **Law of Success**, 2003, Highland Hill Media Group, Los Angeles

Fredrickson, B. L., Cohn, M. A., Coffey, K. A., Pek, J., & Finkel, S. M. Open hearts build lives: *Positive emotions, induced through loving-kindness meditation, build consequential personal resources.* **Journal of Personality and Social Psychology**, 95(5), 1045–1062, 2008

Collins, James C., and Morten T. Hansen. **Great by Choice: Uncertainty, Chaos, and Luck: Why Some Thrive Despite Them All.** 2011, Harper Collins, New York

58936492R00102

Made in the USA
San Bernardino, CA
01 December 2017